T0350352

Automation Max

AUTOMATION MAX

OPTIMIZING AI
AND HUMAN INTELLIGENCE
IN AVIATION

PETER COLLINS

Algora Publishing
New York

© 2020 by Algora Publishing.
All Rights Reserved
www.algora.com

No portion of this book (beyond what is permitted by
Sections 107 or 108 of the United States Copyright Act of 1976)
may be reproduced by any process, stored in a retrieval system,
or transmitted in any form, or by any means, without the
express written permission of the publisher.

Library of Congress Cataloging-in-Publication Data

Names: Collins, Peter (Peter H.), 1957- author.
Title: Automation max: optimizing AI and human intelligence in aviation /
    Peter Collins.
Description: New York: Algora Publishing, [2020] | Summary:
    "Automation-Max outlines the reasons why we should not be making such
    hasty moves towards fully automated passenger aircraft and instead why
    we should start adopting new ideas and concepts to further improve our
    already high standards of aviation safety. In an analysis of the last 10
    years of accidents, the author highlights where the human/computer
    weaknesses lie. He explores the vulnerability of the human pilot in the
    aviation world, and then he takes the debate to the next stage by asking
    how we need to redesign the interface between pilot and machine"—
    Provided by publisher.
Identifiers: LCCN 2020040901 (print) | LCCN 2020040902 (ebook) | ISBN
    9781628944310 (trade paperback) | ISBN 9781628944327 (hardback) | ISBN
    9781628944334 (pdf)
Subjects: LCSH: Airplanes—Automatic control—Safety measures. | Flight
    control. | Human-machine systems. | Aeronautics—Human factors.
Classification: LCC TL589.4 .C57 2020 (print) | LCC TL589.4 (ebook) | DDC
    629.132/6028563—dc23
LC record available at https://lccn.loc.gov/2020040901
LC ebook record available at https://lccn.loc.gov/2020040902

Printed in the United States

To Chantalle, Matthew, Andrew and HAL

Table of Contents

CHAPTER 1: DIGITAL ODYSSEY

A few too many fatal aviation accidents occurred in 2018, going against the expected trend of ever-increasing commercial flight safety. That topic, with an investigation into a Lion Air 737 Max 8 crash that occurred on October 29, 2018, dominated the news program that evening, along with a story on the passing of Douglas Rain. Rain was the actor who provided the voice of HAL in Stanley Kubrick's thought-provoking film *2001: A Space Odyssey*. What an incredible director and what interesting films! I double-checked the viewing schedule for that evening and got lucky when I found out that they had amended the program to re-screen *2001*.

I remembered being intrigued when I first saw that film and frustrated that I couldn't really understand the full meaning behind it. It seemed I would have a chance to see if I could glean anything more, now that I had greater experience in life. Well, I didn't fly for Pan-Am, the airline depicted shuttling passengers to the moon, but I was a captain on the 747-400 and retired before the Pan-Am 001 moon flights became an option on the pilot transfer list. It is notable how the film has turned out to be so accurate in its predictions. This was almost certainly down to the perceptive contributions of a certain Arthur C. Clarke, who wrote the original novel — the present day space station is foreseen; so too is the space shuttle and even a video link system to allow the main protagonist, Dave, to talk to his family through a satellite connection. Furthermore, as I was musing on the scene of Dave talking to his daughter, my solitude was interrupted by a video-chat call from my son.

Just as I was sharing with him this amusing coincidence, my son's face froze and a helpful warning came up, informing me that I had been disconnected. Thank goodness for the message; I would never have guessed. What might have been more helpful would have been a post-call voice message stating, "I detected that a connection fault was imminent and I re-directed to solve the problem. Beware, this could happen at a future time in your current spatial location which may coincide with a critical moment that requires communications and for which I may not have any re-routing options."

Well, actually, an announcement like that would eventually become quite annoying and to be fair to the people that built the internet, they have done a pretty good job, designing various clever protocols that intelligently control the routing and dispersion of our data over the World Wide Web. If a packet of data gets lost in the network, it is re-routed or re-transmitted so it will eventually reach its target destination, albeit a few milliseconds late. The vast majority of these problems occur at "router" pinch points throughout the system or at the end of the line where your device is connecting to the network. If your device is downloading a movie at the same time as handling a conversation over a video chat, the weak link is exposed.

Anyway, back to the film. No, the connection doesn't get dropped with Dave's daughter and yes, the anti-gravity system works just fine for the stewardess. The toilets take a bit of getting used to and the food doesn't look too appetizing, but for a film made in 1968, the predictions are astoundingly accurate. Granted, some of this was borrowed from the research undertaken for the NASA moon-shots and indeed the first navigation system I used in the early Boeing 747s had three of these lunar units.

Neil Armstrong, Buzz Aldrin and Michael Collins all went to the moon with just one of these Inertial Navigation Systems (INS) which was solely responsible for guiding the spacecraft through the three dimensions of space to intercept an object moving at 2,288 miles per hour. On the 747, they gave us three of these INS units as a safety measure in case one went wrong — it's no good having two, because you don't know which one went wrong.

Soon Dave is on his way to Jupiter in another spaceship and we are introduced to "HAL," with his unique style, spookily voiced by Rain. The film to me really seemed to be about this onboard computer system that ran the ship, negating the need for extra crew, much like a commercial pilot does today with no requirement for a Flight Engineer, a Navigator or a Radio Operator. And, as I explained to my son in 21st century parlance, "there's also a monolith that hangs around, sparking off re-birth and stuff."

Arthur C. Clarke predicted the future well. But how are we doing with computer technology in aviation today? The film producers have made many jumps of logic to get HAL up to a very high standard of both ability and reliability, somehow getting us through the present day barrier that has made it so difficult to achieve the expected decline in the number of commercial aircraft accidents.

We'll come back to *2001* later, but for now let's compare some of those accident statistics.

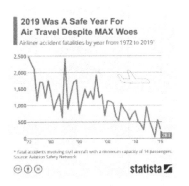

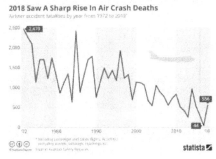

1. *Accident data 2018/9 from Statista*

Starting in 2018, quoting *Statista*, there was a sharp rise in air crash deaths for the year. This book examines that trend to see if there are any clues as to where deficiencies are occurring and how we might improve and/or reinforce any weak points in the system.

Generally, we can consider the table below to represent a realistic indication as to what risks face us in life on our planet at the moment. The odds are approximately one in 188,364 that you will be killed in an aircraft accident.

Cause of Death	Odds of Dying
Heart Disease	1 in 6
Cancer	1 in 7
Chronic Lower Respiratory Disease	1 in 27
Suicide	1 in 88
Opioid overdose	1 in 96
Motor Vehicle Crash	1 in 103
Fall	1 in 114
Gun Assault	1 in 285
Pedestrian Incident	1 in 556
Motorcyclist	1 in 858
Drowning	1 in 1,117

Cause of Death	Odds of Dying
Fire or Smoke	1 in 1,474
Choking on Food	1 in 2,696
Bicyclist	1 in 4,047
Accidental Gun Discharge	1 in 8,527
Sunstroke	1 in 8,912
Electrocution, Radiation, Extreme Temperatures and Pressure	1 in 15,638
Sharp objects	1 in 28,000
Cataclysmic Storm	1 in 31,394
Hot surfaces and substances	1 in 46,045
Hornet, wasp and bee stings	1 in 46,562
Dog attack	1 in 115,111
Passenger on an airplane	1 in 188,364
Lightning	1 in 218,106
Railway passenger	1 in 243,765

2. Lifetime odds of death for selected causes, United States, 2018

As time goes on, you would expect safety to improve, and looking back over the years, this has, on the whole, been the case. Overall the chances of being killed in an airliner are slightly worse than being struck by lightning, so the statistics are not very alarming. However, recently there has been a blip. An article at Inc.com wrote, "Although the global airline industry is rightfully proud of its overall safety record, it's not perfect by any means, and it likely never will be. Here's hoping that the number of deaths in airline accidents drops to zero in 2019."[1] Well, we are now in 2020 and the result for 2019 is 283 deaths according to Statista, which is a great improvement; but we clearly need to keep working on new solutions.

In 2019 the Boeing 737 Max 8 raised questions about the robustness of newly introduced safety systems in 21st-century airliners. Do we even need to train pilots with newly incorporated safety systems — or even inform them that these changes have been introduced into their new aircraft? During this century we may very well be asking how soon we will be able to completely cut out the human from the flight deck to be replaced by computers.

---

[1] https://www.inc.com/peter-economy/there-was-a-stunning-increase-in-airline-crashes-deaths-in-2018-including-a-first-for-southwest.html

---

How ready are we? These are the last 10 years of worldwide passenger aircraft accidents involving fatalities for aircraft certified to carry at least 6 people, including crew. The remaining years going back to 1945 are included in the appendix.

Year	Number of Accidents	Passenger Fatalities
2019	125	578
2018	115	1039
2017	102	399
2016	106	631
2015	127	904
2014	125	1329
2013	141	453
2012	156	800
2011	154	828
2010	162	1154

3. The Bureau of Aircraft Accidents Archives (B3A) accident data 2010–2019

I will be concentrating on airliners that carry at least 14 passengers and on analysis, these accidents fall into specific categories. In the last 10 years (2010–2019) they have ranged from 47 navigation errors to 1 flap-selection error. Some of them seem hard to understand, given the high level of computerization onboard, but maybe there is a limit to the assistance that current computers can provide. We should note at the outset that overall, computer systems have greatly enhanced safety. The rough breakdown of these last 10 years of fatal accidents shows there were 109 serious accidents of which about half could not have been avoided by increased sophistication of aircraft systems. An example of this would be a terrorist bomb or severe mechanical failure.

The question is the reverse: how many such accidents were contributed to by the increased sophistication of aircraft systems, and is this the reason for the statistical blip? We will also ask whether technology itself is sufficiently advanced to start the process of introducing full automation to civil aviation and question whether the current state-of-the-art computer systems alone will have the power and flexibility to replace the human being.

To examine these questions sufficiently, there will be two occasions when I will diversify the discussion to look in more detail at the inner workings of computer processors and also our own biology. These brief interludes encompass our brain's evolution and how well the human can interface with the microprocessor. Finally, we introduce an alternative path of evolution which may produce a more balanced symbiosis between people and machines.

We have already mentioned that computer systems have greatly enhanced aviation safety and there is absolutely no doubt about this. Just how they have done so is interesting, because by looking at the problems they have already solved, we see that their unique selling point was the ability to integrate more effectively with the "human" pilot. As we try to further enhance this integration, we enter the vast grey area that exists between the human thought process and a machine.

There have been several incidents where this grey area has been exposed. A Qantas Airbus A330 (QF 72) was at cruising altitude en route from Singapore to Perth in 2008. The incident report states that the aircraft was flying at 37,000 ft when the autopilot disconnected and the crew received various aircraft system failure indications. Then, shortly afterwards, the aircraft abruptly pitched nose down. The aircraft reached a maximum pitch angle of about 8.4 degrees nose down, and descended 650 ft during the event. After returning the aircraft to 37,000 ft, the crew started the process of actioning the multiple failure messages. The aircraft then commenced a second uncommanded pitch-down maneuver, leaving 12 passengers seriously injured and another 39 requiring hospital medical treatment when it landed, after the subsequent diversion. So what went wrong?

The official report states: "There was a limitation in the algorithm used by the A330 flight control primary computers for processing angle of attack [AOA] data." Effectively, this means an onboard computer suffered an electronic spike and sent invalid data to the control system which blindly pushed the nose down, based on the false notion that the angle of attack had suddenly increased to what it 'thought' was a critical degree.

This is an example of the grey area between the human thought process and a machine. If another linked onboard computer had switched on the seat belt signs, knowing that the aircraft was about to violently pitch down, then I would have been impressed! After several years of flying commercial aircraft and encountering sudden unforecast turbulence, I can definitely recommend that people should keep their seat belts fastened whenever they can!

On Monday, January 1, 2007, an Adamair flight between Surabaya and Manado went missing after its last radio report to Air Traffic Control at 35,000 ft in the cruise. The Inertial Reference System (IRS) malfunctioned and both pilots became preoccupied by attempting to fix the fault and entrusted too much to the automatics/flight computers. The IRS is the next model up from the INS mentioned earlier (the system used by the Apollo astronauts) and is responsible for determining and presenting the orientation (pitch and bank) of the aircraft to the pilots. While the pilots were using their very well evolved human trouble-shooting skills, they switched the IRS units to a warm-up mode called "Attitude" but this caused the autopilot to disengage. For some reason, they ignored and probably cancelled the warning sounds telling them that the autopilot was disengaged, perhaps because they thought the alarm was just a natural consequence of switching to Attitude mode. The aircraft then rolled, unnoticed, 35 degrees to the right, as would be expected at high altitude, and unfortunately the crew were unable to recover the situation, resulting in the loss of all onboard. I wasn't being sarcastic when I said the crew were using their very well evolved human trouble-shooting skills. Pilots are picked for having good problem solving abilities and it wasn't that part of their brain that caused the accident. We will be asking what else we could have done to avoid this accident.

Captain Chesley "Sully" Sullenberger is perhaps the commercial pilot best knoo wn by the wider public since he and his first officer, Jeff Skiles, safely ditched US Airways Flight 1549 in the Hudson River near Manhattan, New York, in January 2009, with no loss of life. The Airbus A320 experienced a total loss of thrust in both engines after encountering a flock of Canada geese encountering a flock of Canada geese in the climbout after takeoff from New York City's LaGuardia Airport. In this whole debate about automation and the future of aviation, Captain Sully has made some interesting and pertinent observations which are especially relevant considering he is widely seen as having outsmarted the automatics. He says:

> It is not easier or cheaper [nor does it] require less training to fly an automated airplane. It frequently requires more, because you have to have a deep understanding of how a system works, including the dark corners, the counterintuitive things it might do in certain circumstances. Many foreign carriers are trying to take people with zero flying experience, put them in simulators and quickly put them in the right seat of a jetliner. They don't have the experience, knowledge, skills and confidence to be the absolute master of the aircraft start to finish.

So another conundrum to solve; the better the automation, the more you need to train the pilots. The airline bosses are thinking and hoping for the exact opposite and are budgeting for lower training costs and crew expenses in an increasingly competitive international industry. More of these types of accident will be analyzed throughout the book and a possible solution is put forward. We also look at whether aviation is a special case or whether there are other industries needing to integrate humans and computers more effectively.

Many commentators are pointing out the problem of "Automation complacency" and the issue of pilot's not having their hands-on skills honed as they would ideally like due to the active encouragement of most airlines for their crews to use the aircraft automatics for the vast majority of the flight. When a serious problem develops on an aircraft, having automatics greatly enhances the chances of a successful outcome but when the automatics go wrong, we then rely upon the extreme skill of the pilot. I guess this will always be a difficult conundrum to solve but our first port of call must be to stop any situation from getting completely out of hand which then leads to the loss of the aircraft. How do we interject at the right moment to break the deadlock and recover when man and machine get out of sync?

My computer odyssey started in 1983 when the first BBC B Micro home computer was produced in the UK and I was flying the Shorts 360 for British Midland Airways out of East Midlands Airport. I learned to write computer programs in BBC Basic and have gone on to write in Assembly code, Visual Basic and Java (Android Applications). I have also happened to have synchronized my flying career with the emergence of digital computer systems on the flight deck and have experienced the advantages and the pitfalls of the airborne microprocessor.

Computers are becoming increasingly sophisticated and we are becoming more detached from the under workings, exposing us to a future where we will be totally reliant on the programmers and more importantly, the companies behind them. I want to demystify the computing process and show it is only a machine following a predetermined set of rules. Although an interesting debate, it doesn't "think" in the same way that you and I might describe the process of "thinking."

The next chapter is the first of the aforementioned digressions and looks at the fundamentals of how computers tick, but like a lot of the content in this book, I have kept the technical aspects to the minimum by covering only the salient points, with the sole intention of exposing what I think is the weak link in the computer microprocessor — the "illusion of thinking."

CHAPTER 2: THINKING COMPUTERS

Safety statistics have at best plateaued over the last few years. One reason may be that we have reached the limitation of the computer systems that have been developing at a rapid pace since the Second World War. To show this, I need to very basically outline how a computer works, but without losing my readership! We need to strip the machine down to the fundamentals to see where any problems lie, just as you would strip an engine down to diagnose a mechanical fault in a car.

The microprocessor is where all the serious action takes place. Forget the rest, the keyboard, monitor (screen), mouse, microphone, speakers, as they either send data to the microprocessor chip or receive data from the microprocessor chip.

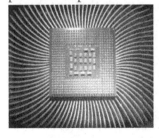 

4. Processor and memory chips

We don't have to consider any of the peripheral parts of the computer; we only need consider the processor and memory chips (above). We also don't need to get tied down by exactitudes in what they are all called (nomenclature). The basics of how it works are surprisingly simple, although the hardware to make it all happen is somewhat more complex.

For those interested in the real fundamentals, I have included a section in the appendix which looks at the very early computer system I once used, the BBC B. It was one of the first personal computers available and, like Stanley Kubrick's *2001*, it was a masterpiece of design. By using its very rudimentary programming language, I will run through the essentials of just how a processor performs its magic, and I think most people will find it interesting. This information is rarely explained, yet it offers an easy to follow insight into the workings of the most abundant machines around us today. All computers and smart phones basically work in the same way. (Quantum computers are a completely different breed and are not included here. They may indeed provide interesting solutions for aviation but this will be way in the future.)

5. *BBC B Personal Computer*

So if you feel adventurous, please have a look at the appendix, "Thinking Computers," to reveal the logic of what is going on inside the thing that is most likely humming away in a corner of your house somewhere. Otherwise, as it is not necessary to have an intimate knowledge of the process, I have précised the contents here.

In summary, the appendix section takes us through the process of adding two numbers together. We see how the first number is represented by a special code sequence and then look at the processor rules applied when the second number is introduced. The two special code sequences (of our two numbers to be added) are superimposed over each other and one by one, the processor rules are activated. Finally, after waiting for a whole ten nanoseconds, the answer reveals itself from the superimposition process, just as invisible ink reveals the character sequence after a special chemical is applied to the secret notepaper.

The reason I'm showing this process is to demonstrate that the computer processor is very mechanical in its behavior — it just does as it's told. It is much like the aforementioned invisible ink, whereby it has the ability to apply the magical special chemical to the paper but it will never understand the meaning of the revealed word or message.

From here, we show how similar processes store the answer into memory so we can retrieve our data for another day, and then follows a brief demonstration of how the processor makes the all-important branching decision. For example, how does the processor determine if one number is larger than another (8 < 17?), which is the essential fundamental, bottom-line ability that any computer must possess in order for it to have any use at all. We experience this ability every day and we call it "choice." This choice then comes into play as we introduce the controlling sequence that is at the heart of all present day computers — the computer program.

To sum up this whole process, the technical explanation of the processor is not really necessary to make the point that a computer is merely moving instructions and data sequentially through the central processor and is very detached from the real world.

The trick is to execute each instruction really quickly, so it appears as if the answer has been produced instantly. Nobody is interested in how many times the Carry Over bit was used just for a very simple addition or how untidy the operation looks. Computers are hyped up to look impressive, but essentially they run streams of data through one pinch point, the processor. Every instruction is handled one by one in a sequential, *series* fashion, and because it works fast it appears to be running in a *parallel* capacity, as does our own human brain. It's much like a magician performing one of those amazing tricks on stage where a person just appears from nowhere. It generally looks a bit suspicious because the cage always has a cloak over it and it's not until the cloak is pulled away that we see the person appear. I still don't know how it's done — but I do know it's a trick.

If I could slow it down, the magician's vulnerability would be exposed because perhaps I would be able to see the person coming up through the trap door. Same too with the computer: if you could slow it down, you would see how it is relying on the sequential codes running in isolation, with interruptions to perform separate tasks, but with no realization of how the tasks are connected. Computers are very good at presenting and crunching data but not so good at interpreting the real world.

Modern day computer games incorporate wonderfully realistic graphics that we can walk through in virtual 3D, and even change in appearance like a Turner painting at sunset as we meander through the landscape in changing sunlight. Flames can flicker in ever increasing realism and we can experi-ence underwater worlds that excite the imagination. But they are not real. They might as well be the individual characters on this page transformed by a machine into a picture. Just like the Turner, the game and the machine, they are merely interpretations made by our parallel, almost 5th dimensional brain.

Microsoft's ubiquitous Windows Operating System has an interesting special feature that gives us a further clue as to the vulnerability of the computer design and how detached computers are from the real world. It's called "Safe Mode" and it's used whenever you, as the human operator, have to help out when the computer gets stuck. The designers know very well that the system is extremely fragile when compared to a human brain and so have installed a safety parachute or a "get out of jail" card. If the computer gets stuck with the little circle going around and around *ad infinitum*, the user has to restart the computer and ensure a special key is pressed on the keyboard so the computer can fire up in a restrained mode whereby it can't retain overall control. The human user then adjusts whatever is necessary and then restarts the machine in normal mode.

A typical problem that computers experience when linked to the internet is virus infection or infiltration. So we install virus checkers to protect us when browsing on the Web; but then some clever criminal designs some malware specifically to uninstall the protective virus checker! So then, as a response, the virus checker manufacturer re-writes the software such that the virus-checker is impossible to uninstall. But perhaps for some reason I independently decide that I want to uninstall the virus checker software myself: and I can't — unless I select "Safe Mode"! What I really need is a computer that offers an "Intelligent Mode"...but I'm afraid it doesn't exist.

The problem is that we are all being seduced into thinking these machines are on the brink of taking over the world, but I would suggest we are on the wrong evolutionary branch and, in aviation, this could be a dangerous supposition, especially as we go through the inevitable transition period to full automation.

After that lot, I think I need a cup of strong black coffee...but how would a computer robot make you a cup of coffee?

CHAPTER 3: COMPUTER LIMITATIONS

Time for that hot cup of coffee. Well, we need to do several things in specific order. It's no good pouring the hot water before we've got the cup on the table.

Basic steps are:

1. Boil some water
2. Get a cup
3. Get a teaspoon
4. Put coffee in cup
5. Pour boiled water into the cup
6. Stir coffee

So imagine we have a centralized computer that has been programmed with the coffee-making instructions. It could feed these instructions to a robot that was suitably equipped with arms and mechanical hands, and probably it would make a cup of coffee for you. Now I will ask the centralized computer to flash this instruction up on a tablet that is being used by a 5-year-old child while I sit back and wait for my coffee. Any problems?

One thing I forgot, you're not allowed to cheat! You're not allowed to use your highly evolved, parallel operating system brain to come up with an abstract, non connected line of logic. The computer can't sense the danger unless you tell it that there is potential problem, in which case you will also have to program in the solution. You as a human being know through masses of parallel neural connections that there is potential for disaster and this is why a computer finds it difficult to operate as we do. Surely, though, we can feed in code to the centralized computer to check it isn't addressing a young child's tablet?

CHECK TABLET REGISTER
IF REGISTERED AGE > 10 THEN CONTINUE
ELSE DO NOT SEND

This tells the computer to check who owns the tablet and if the person's registered age is greater than 10, then that will be acceptable but if not, don't send the message.

Happy now — or have you cheated again? Do we really have to consider the possibility that my child has picked up my wife's tablet?

Interestingly, I find myself grading the dangers.

- Boiling water burn
- Fall off chair getting mug
- Splintered mug causing bodily injury
- Spilt coffee on my brand new carpet

Even if you think the link I've made is slightly tenuous, you will almost certainly agree that it is still a link. Again, the "series" computer system wouldn't have a clue. Only we are tuned in to the wider world, and I would suggest we need to recognize this when designing computer systems for applications that expose us to serious vulnerabilities.

Shall we talk about human failings? Clearly, we have hundreds of them, and in the flying context, we have sadly failed in tragedy after tragedy. But this book is about how we press ahead, seeking to improve matters by harmonizing the human brain with computer systems — we will consider more of this later.

Difficulties with Computer Systems

Quite a while ago, I wrote an Android App which helped monitor saturated fat and calorie consumption by inputting everything you eat in a day and totting it up, to pinpoint which food types are causing the damage and therefore which ones to avoid or control.

To help with the input, you could speak into the device and it would use speech recognition to record the particular food. But although speech synthesis technology is really impressive these days, it did make a few mistakes. Also, I had to consider differences in language like jelly, which in the UK is the wobbly stuff but in America is spread on bread or injected into a doughnut. I'm sure everyone has had a laugh at some of the translations that have come back from speech synthesis programs, which again is an example of the limitations of a "series" system computer. Maybe this is the evolution of what we consider to be a joke or something that is funny — when the brain detects two series calculations arriving at the same neuron cluster, it makes a connection with the laughter motor cortex to convey to others that there is a possible trap that may need to be avoided. Even laughing at a clown tripping over a bucket of water has a sharable lesson. By using my human parallel neuron system, I could enter specific code into my App program that could control things in four ways:

- If the speech returned "pudding," I could exchange the word for "dessert" which the App recognized (covers different words for the same item)
- If the speech returned "you'll get," I could exchange the words for "yoghurt," which the App recognized as the closest match to a food substance
- If the speech returned "Jell-O," I could exchange the word for "jelly," which the App recognized (checks user's language selected in settings)
- If the speech returned something very rude, I could exchange the word for "sausage," "dumplings," or similar to add a bit of humor.

By programming my App in this way I could maintain control over the limitations that otherwise would have rendered the system useless. There were about 1,500 interventions like this in order to control just the foodstuffs that we use on a daily basis.

Another example of how isolated computers can get was demonstrated after the dreadful events in Christchurch, New Zealand, in 2019, where a lone shooter was able to live-stream the atrocity over social media. Obviously, the company concerned would never have sanctioned this but it took a human to realize what was happening and take it down. This situation is similar to what can occur on a flight deck where we need the computer itself to make timely critical decisions, pertinent to the real world emergency, and then act upon them independently so as to properly safeguard the aircraft.

Internet fraud is another scourge on society with countless examples of people innocently working away on-line and then finding that the operating system code, far from protecting them, is actually incapable of detecting some fraudulent attacks that end up causing untold misery. For example, when buying a car in the UK, you can enter the registration details into a special government-run website which tells you if the car you are about to purchase has been involved in a serious accident and therefore could have been dangerously reconstructed, or at least should be available for a lower price. But again, like passing the coffee-making instructions to a 5-year-old child, the system fails because now we are relying on other parties to register the accident in the first place, which unsurprisingly doesn't always happen. We are led to believe that the computer system is intelligent and protecting us.

Is it fair to say then that a computer is just a fast idiot? There is some truth there, somewhere, I think, but I might rephrase to say that it is doing the very best job it can and that we get many, many advantages from the processor; but we should not be over-reliant on the manufacturers who want us to keep buying their latest systems... especially when it comes to safety.

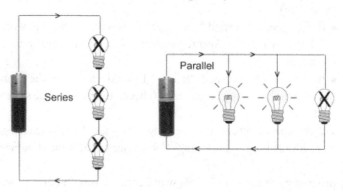

6. *Electric circuits — Series, all bulbs fail; Parallel, one bulb fails*

Nature and electromagnetism provide a classic example of where one solution may lie, specifically in consideration of electrical circuits. You may be familiar with this from college whereby you set up two types of circuit, one series and one parallel. Indeed, you may be familiar with it from trying different strings of Christmas tree lights.

If one bulb blows in the series circuit, the other two bulbs are cut off from the electron supply and so all the bulbs fail — total system failure. However, if a bulb blows in the parallel circuit, although the electrons cannot pass through the faulty bulb, they can pass through the other bulbs by taking the alternative route at the wire junction and so the majority of the system remains active.

On an airliner the Takeoff Configuration warning system is an example of a "series" system. The idea is that if the pilots forget to put the flaps down for takeoff, which increases the lift on the wing and allows the aircraft to get airborne before the runway runs out, an alarm sounds inside the flight deck. This is a very clever idea and has saved many lives over the years, so I'm definitely not knocking it; but at least two accidents have occurred when aircraft fitted with the system have attempted to get airborne with no flaps. The system is triggered when the pilot opens the thrust levers or throttles for takeoff and, on passing through a certain point, a switch is engaged which checks if the flaps are down. If not, the alarm sounds and the pilot is able to safely abandon the takeoff.

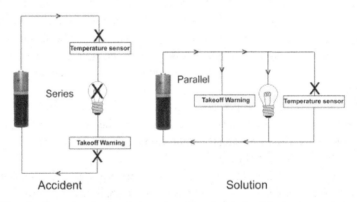

The takeoff warning circuit remains active with an isolated or defective temperature sensor

This unfortunately happened to Spanair Flight 5022 that crashed just after takeoff from runway 36L at Madrid Airport on August 20, 2008. I will discuss this more fully in a later chapter but briefly, the pilots had a technical fault on taxi out, whereby a temperature sensor was overheating and returned to the gate to have it fixed. The fix involved shutting down the circuit for the temperature sensor (pulling a circuit breaker) which was unfortunately in series with the Takeoff warning system, and as a result of the crew now being late, a human error crept in whereby they forgot to run the checklists and lower the flaps for takeoff. Now, no warning was available and the aircraft crashed as it attempted to get airborne with insufficient lift — resulting in 154 casualties.

Why don't they just wire everything in parallel? Because the amount of connections would be impracticable due to the quantity of wires involved, and if you could do so, you wouldn't be able to carry a full load of passengers and freight due to the excessive weight of wires and connectors!

One safety measure that utilizes a parallel system has been developed in conjunction with the arrival of very long haul flight operations; it is what is called the "Heavy." This refers to the heavy pilot, who is required to be part of the crew (heavily-loaded crew — one more than required to fly the aircraft) because of one of the many human failings, "sleep deprivation." We all know that human performance diminishes with fatigue, so not a good idea doing the most demanding part of the flight, namely the landing, after flying for twelve hours. So the heavy pilot helps by running the flight in cruise, thus allowing the two operating pilots to take turns to rest for one third of the flight (always ensuring there are 2 pilots at the controls at any one time). The extra bonus is that the "Heavy" can observe the crucial elements of the takeoff and landing and in the Spanair case could have spotted that the flaps had not been extended. He is only looking for what hasn't been completed or what has been missed and therefore is not as preoccupied as the operating pair. Why don't we have a heavy pilot on each flight? Cost to the airlines, say no more.

But what about parallel computers, artificial intelligence, machine learning and cluster computers? These sound like the next generation solutions, and as we are addressing the limitations of the series computer, surely the parallel computer is the answer?

As we have mentioned earlier (and in the appendix), parallel computers are the result of Moore's Law coming to a grinding halt. Moore's Law asserts that the number of transistors on a microchip doubles every two years. Well, up until the microchip began to melt, that was correct. Another lesson here — maybe let's not be in such a hurry to put undue reliance on forward predictions until they have been thoroughly tested by time. Moore himself, to be fair, thought there would be a limit to his law, but the wider world seemed to be less cautious about future predictions, the pitfalls of which the pharmaceutical industry has learned to its cost over the years. So now we have included two (or more) processors to share the work and thus halve the heat given off. But the designers now have another problem in that they need to tell the computer how to share the work. In effect, it has now become more complicated and arguably, potentially more prone to error.

Parallel Computers

There are different ways that this parallel computing can be achieved. We'll just consider using two processors for simplicity.

- Multiprocessing — Both processors execute a program each and the two separate answers are available at the end. E.g. one adds sales numbers, the other counts up the stock. No need for any correlation at the processing stage.
- Parallel processing — there is only one program but the programmer writes it such that one processor does some parts and the other processor does others. E.g., one adds sales numbers, the other counts the stock. At the end, the program uses both sets of data to make a useful prediction.
- Data parallelism — when there is one program and it has to process a huge amount of data, so it sends half the data to one processor and the other half to the other processor. E.g., one counts the stock at the London factory; the other counts the stock at Manchester. At the end, the program uses both sets of data to list total stock.

So this is like requiring a steam train to ascend a steep gradient. One huge locomotive won't be as efficient as two smaller ones (due to the increased weight) and therefore, essentially, they are both the same old locomotives we know and love that come with all the weaknesses and problems, except I now have to synchronize them to ensure they are pulling together as one. Communication and synchronization are big problems with parallel computing. The programs need to be written so they can handle the parallel structure.

Cluster Computers

Cluster computers use two or more computers that are networked together to facilitate the ability to utilize parallel computing. Networking is where two computers are linked by a cable or Wi-Fi. This set up typically would be used to back up files from one computer to the other. But by clustering them, the principle of parallel computing can now be utilized, whereby the two processors share the work required, run by a complex synchronizing program operating in the background.

Machine Learning and Artificial Intelligence

Machine learning is a way in which we can train a computer to be artificially intelligent. Take face recognition. You feed the computer thousands of face images and run your program designed to use many different ways of deciding on how to interpret a face. A lump in the middle is a nose, two sockets top left and right for eyes, etc. Now make hundreds of these rules and then sit a subject in front of a camera ready for the computer to compare her or his face to the photo file held on the disk storage system. When the computer gets it right, the rules that were primarily responsible for supplying the correct answer get a star, just like you would give to a child at primary school. Now, those favorable algorithms are brought into play more aggressively to improve the overall hit rate and thus the success rate of the system.

Although we are merely mimicking the learning process of a young human brain, this does have huge potential for the future. I could not sift through thousands of camera shots of people and match them to a villain's mug shot. I could do about fifty but no more, and that is where the computer does very well — it can do millions.

This same ability is exploited by autopilot computers to keep an airliner flying straight and level at altitude. It is very demanding for a pilot to fly a heavy airliner at precicely 35,000 ft without autopilot assistance because of what is called the damping effect. I certainly couldn't do it for hours on end. All pilots engage an autopilot and rely on the very fast calculations and reactions of the computer system to maintain the required altitude. The damping effect problem is caused by the less dense air at altitude and is similar to how a car's suspension works.

In a vehicle with hard springs or shock absorbers, any disturbance from a pot hole in the road is very quickly rectified by the powerful springs (equivalent to the thick air at low altitude). With soft springs, it takes longer for the disturbance to settle down as the springs go back and forth several times before they stabilize the car (equivalent to the thin air at high altitude).

Machine Learning and Artificial Intelligence do repetitive tasks very well, learning all the way, but it is extremely difficult to transpose it into a similar but different task. Other uses for artificial intelligence are: speech recognition, medical diagnosis, stock market trading, analyzing buying habits/associations, classification into groups, financial services /prediction on loan default. In all of these, the same applies; it does a repetitive task very well but can be relied upon for doing just that ONE task without a lot of reprogramming. The medical AI diagnosis program works very well at spotting lung cancer cells off a scan, but that's where it ends. It is a very helpful tool, but we maybe should be careful about labeling it as Artificial "Intelligence."

The analogy with children holds well here, in that you can teach a child to tell a joke, but that doesn't mean that child can tell that joke to anyone at any time — it has to learn what "appropriate" means — and that is a high level skill for a human; in fact, it is still debated today how we do this ourselves. We don't yet have the answer.

Cortana, Siri, Alexa...

Are these systems using artificial intelligence? They call them weak AI, as it can recognize abstract patterns and meanings. For instance — "What's going down at the club tonight" is recognized as "what is happening at the club tonight," without realizing there is an embedded suggestion of a crime or a deal. It appears that these systems don't *think*, they just recognize certain patterns. I'm inclined to believe that once we have sorted out what we mean by "thinking" we can then make a start on programming a computer to match the concept; until then, let's not use the word "think" in the same sentence as the word "computer."

Warnings on Flight Decks

Another challenge with computers in aircraft is the output. How does the computer communicate with the pilots? Currently we have a Crew Alerting System that either speaks or flashes a message up on a prominent monitor, coupled with a warning chime to get the crew's attention. These are all graded by a human programmer. If the aircraft is approaching high ground at a dangerous altitude, the system will:

- Call out, "TERRAIN, TERRAIN."
- Sound a warning claxon.
- Flash up the words TERRAIN on the central monitor in red capital letters.
- Offer guidance on the pilot flight displays as to what angle of climb is required to avoid the obstacle.

This will definitely get your attention but what happens when a whole series of things go wrong? This happened when a Qantas A380 departed Singapore and an engine exploded, damaging the leading edge high lift devices as well as many other systems in and around the engine. As far as the computer was concerned, it had done its job really well by informing the pilots that there were multiple disagreements between several systems and maybe also that the toilet-occupied light was not working! We don't really want to know about the toilet light at the moment, but we do want to know the condition of the leading edge flap. The computer could not "intelligently" discern the difference.

The human would look at the leading edge and importantly ignore the superfluous warnings, knowing that by getting involved with these distractions would only further confuse the situation, eventually leading to an information overload and the possible loss of the aircraft. The Qantas crew sorted the situation out brilliantly and were able to analyze and action each computer fault readout, one by one (you resolve each line on the aircraft's MCDU computer), and importantly, ensuring the critical ones were dealt with first.

Conclusion

If the aim is to track millions of peoples' online buying habits or to assist the police using face recognition software, we can afford to experiment with the systems and see whether they work in the long run. But on a flight deck we need to be clear about what we are trying to achieve. Perhaps the rules should be:

- Positively encourage machines that assist the human with repetitive actions.
- Don't try to replace the human brain yet, design systems to integrate more effectively with the human being.

I worry about the use of parallel computing and artificial intelligence in aviation, as we could be unknowingly led into introducing them too quickly, imagining they are actually mimicking the human brain. Thinking is a multiple parameter function, and it's very difficult to mimic in a series style computer.

The successful partnership of the human brain and the series computer appears to have peaked, as accident statistics have climbed again. In order to get back on track, we need an improved symbiosis of human and computer.

We are all familiar with this visualization of how mankind evolved from the apes:

7. Visualization of human evolution

But, of course, this image is not really correct and it can only be considered as an artistic interpretation — a better representation of these characters would be this:

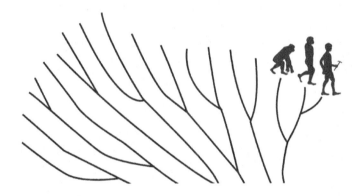

8. More accurate visualization of human evolution

The essential part is that as evolution progresses, it branches out from the last lineage. Apes branched off from monkeys about 25 million years ago, which then branched into the Great Apes, and finally the chimpanzees branched into humans, still leaving the chimps to play their part in our world today, pretty much so as they have always done. The evolutionary process doesn't mean one form gradually morphs into the new species; it picks the right time and then branches off when it's ready — if it gets it wrong, then the lineage ceases to be.

I'm always amused by thoughts of evolution and the opposing argument of the existence of a God. One side says a God created man and the other side says man simply evolved. But the evolutionists are always quick to add that at no stage was there any intelligent intervention, it was all trial and error and random selection. The amusing part is imagining all the failed attempts by nature along the way, and in this context you can imagine how "serial brain" man would have fared. With a spear inbound, serial man would have to decide when to hand over control from visual tracking to muscle reaction so he could take evasive action to avoid the spear. By controlling these two functions simultaneously, our evolutionary branch was able to react much faster, and that is why a tennis player can today react to a serve received at 150 mph and still win the point! Sure, you can incorporate fast interrupts in the serial processor, but there is more to run in the body other than sight and muscle movement; so series humans would never have got the better of our Sapiens brain architecture.

We should keep trying to improve series style computers, but if we assume that we have evolved sufficiently to be at the branch-off point to full automation, we risk relying on a system that is pretty good but somewhat awkward in its habitat. At the right time, we can branch off from the series computer lineage into a human-like neural network design, and only then should we consider handing over full control to digital systems.

Chapter 4: Benefits of Computers Onboard

When I first started operations on the 747 Classic (the original jumbo jet), we used the same Inertial Navigation Systems (INS) that the first men on the moon used for navigation, except they only had one. Up until then, we followed various types of radio beacons that pointed to a geographical location. The needle would point up at twelve o'clock on the dial until you arrived at the beacon, and then it would rotate very quickly (if you were good at tracking) around the dial until it was pointing to 6 o'clock as you passed overhead. With the INS, the computer knew where you were at any time, and geographically named locations weren't really required anymore. They did keep them on charts, though, so that Air Traffic Control could radio transmit an easy way of directing aircraft, and the "waypoint" was invented.

Now all I had to do was tell the computer which waypoints I wanted to follow. In the early days, the system could only take latitude and longitude, which meant typing in something like this: N15032.0W01045.6

And very annoyingly, it could only accept 10 entries at a time. Even more annoying, it was found that mistakes could easily be made by entering an incorrect digit and the aircraft could unexpectedly set course for Australia or Timbuktu. To get over this, it became airline policy for one other flight deck crew member to double check the entry — in those days the crew comprised a captain, first officer and flight engineer. After the digit entries were made, the computer would calculate the angles between the tracks (at least the first angle, as the world is round) and the distance. This was then checked off against a printout that was prepared specially for each flight — a cross-check system.

When the Flight Management System (FMS) upgrade arrived, all the pilots who had grown up with computers saw this as a massive improvement, although for others it required quite a learning curve. But as the diversification was purposely designed to be limited, everybody caught on quickly. This is where the computer excels: for us, no more tedious Lat/Long entries to be made, and more important, far fewer mistakes. And by increasing the memory of the computer, we could now store one- to five-letter names instead of 15-digit Lat/Longs. There were names like WOOLY, that could be easily reproducible as they were chosen to sound like an English word. The FMS had a much larger memory and what's more, a look-up database that would store the waypoint names and their geographical Lat/Long coordinates. This improved safety in two main ways: •

- The Lat/Long of WOOLY was hard-wired into the memory, so not much room for error.
- If the pilot mistakenly typed WOOLI, the FMS would display a "Not Found" message instead of setting course for Wooloomaloo.

Still, though, problems could occur. What would happen if there was another waypoint in the world called WOOLY? This happened to American Airlines Flight 965 in December 1995 in Cali, Columbia, when the pilots became disorientated and decided to break the confusion by flying back to a beacon called "R" (Romeo), to recommence the approach. They read the name "R" off their letdown charts, so they knew it was the correct beacon. But this particular beacon had been in conflict with another beacon near Bogota with the same name ("R"), so the authorities changed the name of the Cali beacon to ROZO — but the letdown charts hadn't been updated. Obviously with so many waypoints around the world, there are bound to be some conflicts, but this eventuality had been taken into account by the FMS designers; if there were two ROZO beacons or two "R" waypoints, then the system would list both with their Lat/Longs and then invite the pilot to pick the correct one.

So far, in the context of this book, the logic handling is not too bad. Furthermore the FMS designers added another step of logic to help the pilot pick the correct beacon identifier. The possibilities were listed in order of how close they were to the aircraft. It is quite challenging for anyone to work this out mentally, using just latitude and longitude, especially under pressure. The computer does really well here — apart from one thing. The pilot assumed that the top selection of "R" was the closest beacon, as was the design — and it wasn't. The one he wanted wasn't even there, as it had been changed to ROZO. The one he selected was the one near Bogota and the aircraft was duly turned by the autopilot towards Bogota, with a 9,800 ft mountain in the way. This was the classic Swiss cheese problem: there are always holes in the system. Here, the incorrect chart notification lined up perfectly with a momentary confusion in situational awareness.

The Swiss cheese analogy has been used in aviation for a while — if the holes in each slice of Swiss cheese line up perfectly when stacked on top of each other in a sandwich, there is now a potential way through for the mayonnaise to make a mess on one's shirt. The idea is to arrange the slices so no holes are aligned, and in aviation the simplest example is a checklist. The holes start to line up if we rely on memory to lower the flaps for takeoff. The checklist helps block the mayonnaise but the alignment isn't guaranteed to be perfect, as we can still forget to read the checklist.

The improvement with the FMS was very welcomed but another issue appeared. Once introduced, several of us made suggestions about how we could add more data to the system to make the operation even smoother, but the reply from Boeing was a very early acknowledgement of the issue being discussed in this book. If you make any changes to the system, hidden, unknown consequences could appear during the normal operation of the FMS so there would need to be rigorous testing time allocated to re-certify the software. This was costly and impracticable.

There is no doubt about it, computers have made a huge contribution to safety in aviation; but to go to the next stage of full automation, we will need computers to become a conscious part of the operation and not just be a useful tool in the toolbox. At Cali, can it be argued that had the aircraft not had the FMS, the pilots would have done things the old-fashioned way and dialed up the frequency from the chart on the radio box to follow the needle to the correct "R" beacon? Undoubtedly, but this would be easily counter-acted by many examples of where a database system has plugged the Swiss cheese holes and prevented an accident from occurring, let alone without considering the contributions from all the other computerized systems onboard a modern airliner.

On a four-engine aircraft, you used to get an irritating beating noise as the sound waves from the low pressure fans at the front of the engines interfered with each other. But computers now keep all the four engines running at exactly the same revolutions per second to minimize the noise. Before, we would have to look up takeoff power settings from graphs and tables to work out the correct thrust setting for the engines, which then needed constant monitoring as the aircraft climbed into thinner air. Now the FMS computer takes in all the necessary data and displays the current target on the EICAS

(Engine Indication and Crew Alerting System). Furthermore, with the autothrust system, the computer ensures optimum thrust at all times and, importantly, during a go-around when timely application of increased thrust is essential. These comforting add-ons to the aircraft systems make the job much easier — but what if pilots ever found themselves in a situation where the Thrust Reverse system was not working: what would happen then?

Well, it's important to think laterally when considering service issues like these, as there could be some unusual consequences that could affect the safety of the flight. If a thrust reverser was not in working order on a 747, the jet would still be permitted to take off, but it would be essential to consider what would happen if the takeoff was to be rejected. In this case, provided the runway isn't too slippery, the aircraft is perfectly controllable with only three reversers working and this maneuver is practiced in simulators twice yearly. The problem is that the brakes won't work very well in slippery conditions and the reverse thrust would now be asymmetric, causing the aircraft to slide to the side of the runway. So, fine for departure on a dry runway, but what if the destination runway is covered in snow? In that case, the aircraft won't be permitted to operate that particular flight, and the airline would have to fix the problem; but if this were not possible, we would consult a very thick manual that crosschecks every combination and possible consequence of just about every conceivable failure. Inside this defects manual, we would see that — provided there were no other associated failures or critical runway conditions — we would be permitted to operate the aircraft.

We would have dealt with an unserviceable autothrottle system in the same way. Autothrottle is the system that sets the required thrust setting throughout the flight and, by checking the thick manual, we would have found that operating with "manual throttles" would have been permissible. So instead of the computer setting the required thrust, we would simply push or pull the thrust levers to the required setting.

How would an unserviceable autothrottle system work with full automation? For a start, the defects manual will be surprisingly thin since, with no pilots onboard, each departing aircraft would have to be in pretty much perfect order. Pilots can fly aircraft without an autothrottle, but it's a bit much to ask of an automatic aircraft!

This brings up the two different philosophies of Boeing and Airbus. The Boeing philosophy allows the aircraft to be flown without an autothrottle. Airbus also allows the aircraft to be flown without an autothrottle (autothrust system) though is generally not recommended by most airlines. The difference is that on the Airbus, the autothrust system will switch back in to recover the aircraft if taken outside of the permitted flight envelope. Airbus have made a good attempt at designing a fully automatic autothrust system but vulnerabilities can still exist, with pilots both in and out of the loop.

And when might one of these deficiencies show up? It would be nice, would it not, if your car only went wrong when it's been in the garage all night? The real world doesn't work that way, and normally breakdowns occur whilst out on the road. How does full automation deal with this one? For a start, there will be huge delays as ground engineers go about their business maintaining the aircraft to near perfect condition, and then we will all have to hope that the autothrottle (amongst many other systems) doesn't develop a fault en route.

In days gone by, this issue would never have cropped up because there was no automatic thrust system — it was just the normal operating procedure. So pilots today have to learn another set of procedures — one with the automatics and one without. Nowadays, with pilots being mainly accustomed to flying the aircraft in automatic mode, it is easy to revert and assume the autothrottle will be looking after the speed control during the landing approach, when in fact it may remain unserviceable. This is one of those *dark corners* Captain Sully was talking about earlier.

Asiana Airlines Flight 214 was landing at San Francisco International in 2013 when it had a related accident. The 777 was being radar vectored to land on runway 28L and, as any regular aviator to KSFO knows, Air Traffic Control is liable to keep you high on the approach phase of the arrival due to the proximity of several other airports. It even has a nickname amongst pilots, named after a basketball scoring technique — a slam dunk. The Asiana flight was also high, and when this occurs on any aircraft, the thrust needs to be reduced to minimum (flight idle) so the aircraft can descend as quickly as possible onto the correct glide angle and without building up too much speed. At some stage, the operating captain on Asiana 214 selected an automatic mode that was good for a rapid descent but resulted in the disconnection of the autothrottle — so now he needed to be in the "automatics out" mindset.

When the aircraft was on very short finals, just about to land, the 777 had regained the correct glide angle required for landing. But the crew were subconsciously expecting the autothrottle to then maintain the required approach and landing speed; and now that the nose had been raised to follow the correct glide path, the speed bled off to critically low levels. The aircraft didn't make it to the runway and the tail section hit a seawall, killing 3 people.

If there is good crew communication on a flight deck, every button press is announced out loud so everybody knows what has just been switched on or off and more importantly to alert everybody to the potential consequences that may not manifest themselves until much later on in the flight. Just about all computers systems are a benefit onboard, but because they can't think for themselves, they often need supervision.

Hong Kong was a place where the autothrottle was most useful. That is, in the days of Kai Tak (the old, now disused airport), which involved a 47 degree last-minute, low-level turn to land. Because of the steep mountainous terrain surrounding Kai Tak, the only way in was down an offset ILS (Instrument Landing System), towards checkerboard hill, which was quite literally a red and white checkered pattern painted on a hillside. It was there to warn you that there was a certain urgency to start the turn NOW! Once the turn was complete, the aircraft would be lined up with the runway at an altitude of about 200 ft with little time for correction if you had misjudged the turn. The autothrottle was immensely useful during the turn as it would keep the speed spot-on, whilst the pilot was executing and correcting the turn in the variable wind, following the curved, flashing lead in lights.

The latter part of the route to Hong Kong was also notorious for summoning up dense areas of thunderstorm activity (CB). A great advantage of the new glass cockpits was that they came with the weather radar interlinked and superimposed over the Navigation Display. Now we had a picture of the route ahead, and on top were the color coded weather returns showing exactly where we would encounter the thunderstorms. The color coding was the same used on typical TV weather channels today, where the purple colors are the most intense, going down through red, yellow and green. This was especially useful at night when normally only a lightning flash would provide any visual feedback as to the relative position of the CBs and their anvil tops that frequently crossed the flight path.

The INS/IRS navigation systems used for calculating the aircraft position (and thus navigation) are extremely accurate but they do drift with time. These units are started on the ground during the pre-flight checks; the current latitude and longitude are inserted and after about 10 minutes, the 3 perpendicular platforms will align and therefore be available to accurately detect any minute movements of the aircraft. These movements are measured by accelerometers on the 3 level platforms which, once fed into a computer, calculate the position (Lat and Long) as well as the speed of the aircraft. In the early days, the drift rate was about 2 nautical miles per hour; now is much improved, at about 0.6 nautical miles per hour. However, today they are linked in to the GPS and so are continually updated to maintain the aircraft position to within 15 meters accuracy. Now we have another problem.

The GPS is so accurate that if two aircraft were flying in opposite directions at the same height on the same airway, they would most probably collide. There are rules about flight levels in airways and so this shouldn't occur, but if one aircraft has an emergency and needs to descend, there could be a near miss or worse. To get round this one, most airlines now fly an offset whereby the pilot's instruct the flight computers to purposely fly with an error of one nautical mile to the right of track. So now if two aircraft were in error at the same level, flying in opposite directions, they should pass each other with a lateral separation of 2 nm.

Situation awareness has been a longstanding aviation term and can be described as how the human brain interprets the exact state of the aircraft at any one time and the projection of how this state will change over time. It is an essential element of a pilot's operation and has been greatly helped by onboard computers.

VNAV stands for Vertical Navigation and is used from top of descent to landing. A 747-400 will take about 5 miles to slow down from 300 kts to 250 kts with the thrust levers closed. The irony of a large airliner is that, due to its huge momentum (speed x weight), if all the engines fail at altitude it will take much longer to reach the ground than a smaller aircraft. In normal operations the VNAV computer system will predict ahead, showing graphically on the pilot's navigation display the exact point on the predicted routing where the aircraft will be at the desired height and speed.

The displays for the pilots are game changing in that they interface with the human pilot in a more meaningful way showing a clear picture of the route the aircraft is following and compacting all the important flight information, like height, speed, climb rate, etc. into one display. This helps the pilot scan for information more efficiently, and this frees up more spare brain capacity for when it may be needed. Large liquid crystal display (LCD) screens provide a clear logical diagram of systems like fuel tank state, which helps when deciding on how to ensure the fuel is balanced, lessening the risk of switching off the wrong fuel pump and causing a pilot-induced problem.

Computers are now providing head-up displays that help the pilot see out of the front windshield in a "virtual" way in which she would naturally see if the clouds were not blocking the view. It also provides essential flight information, projected over the windshield like airspeed, altitude and rate of descent.

Autopilots are another safety feature that don't quite count in this digital context but, interestingly, are misunderstood by most passengers. It can be thought that passengers are safer if the pilot is actually flying the aircraft, but by releasing the human brain from repetitive actions, it improves the overall safety by many hundreds of percent. I remember seeing a video clip of an Antarctic explorer being interviewed on board an airliner; he was travelling home and recounting how extreme the conditions had been whilst working outside in the snow and he commented on how nice it was to be in normal surroundings. Outside air temperature was minus 70 degrees C, and the atmosphere outside would render him unconscious in 30 seconds due to lack of oxygen; his momentum was dangerously high; he was at 35,000 ft balancing on a metal wing full of explosives, with engines running at 700 degrees C, with a CB in the vicinity that could throw the aircraft inside out and upside down! But it's good that passengers are generally very relaxed about flying...

Autopilots have been around for a long time. They used to be run by analogue computers that literally had only one task to perform — they weren't connected to a microchip processor. Same goes for fly-by-wire, which is common nowadays but of course the Wright brothers used wires to control the Kitty Hawk, so they don't really count as a contribution towards enhanced safety. Fly-by-wire is a system that replaces the conventional cables that run from the flight deck to the control surface motors of the aircraft (rudder, aileron and elevators). A computer system now sends an electrical signal to the motor which moves the control surfaces, providing several benefits. The electrical wires are much lighter than the cables, jammed cables are no longer a concern and the computer can now interpret the pilot's control inputs to ensure the aircraft is kept within the allowable flight envelope. However, there are arguments that a severe lightening strike could severely degrade the entire aircraft control system but it hasn't happened yet. In 2019, a Sukhoi airliner crashed on landing at Moscow–Sheremetyevo airport having returned after a reported lightening strike shortly after departure. I await the accident report to see if there were any issues with the flight controls as the aircraft was equipped with a Fly-by-wire system.

No pilot can manually land an aircraft safely in foggy weather conditions without the assistance of Autoland. It's been around since the 1960s. Because the weather in Great Britain has always been prone to anticyclonic gloom and fog, Autoland was primarily developed by British European Airways (BEA), the major UK short haul carrier. The first commercial automatic landing, carrying passengers, was achieved on flight BE 343 on June 10, 1965, and was a Trident 1 on a flight from Paris to Heathrow.

This was a genuine benefit of computers onboard but, of course, since we're talking about 1965, it did not involve digital computers. They utilized analogue systems that were coupled into the ILS beams emanating from the landing runway. The ILS (Instrument Landing System) has two beam components, one lateral and one vertical. The lateral beam guides the aircraft's left/right alignment towards the runway and the vertical beam guides the descent angle, so that the aircraft will touch down about 1000 ft in from the runway threshold. The system knows when to flare the aircraft (for a gentle touchdown) by a link to the radio altimeter, which is a much more accurate instrument compared to the regular barometric altimeters. The aircraft has to be flown by the autopilot, as a human pilot cannot correctly interpret the strange appearance of the runway as it reveals itself at 140 miles per hour through dense fog. It was too risky to trust only one autopilot with this critical maneuver and so three were used, each continually comparing itself to the other two to check for faults.

This same type of system is widely used today and runs off separate, independent computer systems in the aircraft. But there are still times when a human needs to get involved. If there are strong winds at the landing airfield, exceeding 25 kts (the 747-400's limit), then the Autoland won't be available because the system is unable to handle the more erratic flight path generated by the strong winds. Humans can read ahead and predict the sometimes significant flight path deviations far better than the computer, but if the runway is covered in a blanket of fog, it's time to divert. If the visibility on the runway is less than 100 meters, then again the Autoland is not approved. To be fair to the system, this is only because the fire services would be unable to locate the aircraft in the event of an emergency on the runway — the Autoland has no concept of visibility, as was referenced in the expression "blind landing." During the approach it is essential that the pilots closely monitor the ILS indicators that display the lateral and vertical displacement of the aircraft from the ideal flight path. If a large aircraft is taxiing out to take off and is close to the landing runway, the hull of the taxiing aircraft can distort the ILS beams like a lens distorts light in a magnifying glass. This can seriously affect an aircraft carrying out an Autoland and so Air Traffic Control need to declare Low Visibility Procedures (LVPs). This means they have to ensure taxiing aircraft are kept well away from the ILS beams. Finally, if things go awry, it is always the pilot's decision to abort the landing and carry out a go-around; the automatics don't have the insight to make these sorts of decisions.

Another area of importance is the Crew Alerting System where any onboard system faults are communicated to the pilots. Years ago, if a temperature sensor on an engine registered an overheat, it would be transmitted through a wire to the flight deck where it terminated at a bulb. Etched into the bulb cover was the word "overheat," so when the light came on, the pilot could see it was an overheat, and because it was the second light in from the right, it was the number 3 engine. Now, with cathode ray tubes (CRT) and LCDs, the indication can be squeezed in to make the presentation more concise. This is a major advantage.

The picture below of the 747 flight decks shows how less cluttered the flight deck has become. Note the extra flight engineer aboard the 747 Classic.

9. Boeing 747 Classic and 747-400 flight decks

There are traps here, as well. British Midland Flight 92, a Boeing 737-400, crashed onto the motorway embankment between the M1 motorway and the A453 road near Kegworth, Leicestershire, UK, in 1989. The left engine had failed but the crew shut down the other engine as a result of 3 main lines of logic:

- The air-conditioning on older 737 aircraft was fed from the right engine and the presence of smoke in the flight deck led the captain to think it was the right engine that had therefore failed. They were flying a later model of 737 where both engines fed the A/C system.
- When the supposed bad engine was shut down by the F/O, it coincided with a level off at the cleared altitude and the subsequent throttle back reduced both the engine vibration and also the amount of smoke entering the flight deck, which reconfirmed the initial diagnosis.
- The new instrumentation on the 737-400 aligned the secondary engine instrument readouts (including the vibration indicators) on the right hand side of the flight panels as shown below.

10. The secondary engine instrument readouts located on the right hand side of the instrument panels.

This third point also reconfirmed the initial diagnosis that the vibration was from the right side, as they were seeing the warning being displayed on the right hand side of the flight deck panels. In fact they were seeing the left engine display, although both gauges were situated on the right of the panel. A classic Swiss cheese. In order to help improve the situation, it was now seen that the displays should be re-designed, where possible, to show a clear left/right disparity when considering major systems of the aircraft.

We have already discussed the issue of modern crew alerting systems and looked at the Qantas flight out of Singapore. We need to try and solve the issue of excessive warnings spilling out into the flight deck — how do we get the system to tell us what we need to know as opposed to absolutely everything that the system is currently sensing?

There are three basic levels of warning used in an airliner. The really important warnings of an engine fire rings a bell, displays a message in RED capitals, shines a red light on each relevant component and brackets the engine indications. These need to be dealt with immediately. The next level is a Caution, like an electrical generator fault. These light up in amber and with four of them fitted on a 747, it is not really an issue but action is necessary. After that there are the Advisory warnings like "high brake temperatures" which might pop up after a landing on a short runway, giving the pilot information on conditions that could present a problem if ignored.

Good to have all the input; but what if I desperately need to know one tiny piece of information amongst a maelstrom of sound and flashing lights?

Air France 447 was flying from Rio de Janeiro, Brazil, to Paris, and crashed on June 1, 2009. The Airbus A330 was at cruising altitude and low speed stalled all the way down, eventually crashing into the Atlantic Ocean, killing all 228 passengers and crew on board. If I could have beamed myself aboard, I would have only had to shout 3 words, "LOW SPEED STALL." The captain, who had been on his crew rest rotation and was suddenly called upon to sort out the confusion, would have then realized that the power urgently needed to be increased, ignoring the illusion of over speeding as reported by the Primary Flight Display. One tiny fault had triggered a whole mass of sensory warnings and none of them told the captain what he needed to know. Just to note, it is also possible to have a high speed stall. The curved top surface of the wing induces the air to whip over the wing even faster than the aircraft is actually flying and if the aircraft is approaching the sound barrier (at altitude the sound barrier can be relatively close) the shock wave will form on the wing top surface before anywhere else and cause a breakdown in the airflow, inducing loss of lift together with a lot of vibration. The same vibration is experienced with a slow speed stall whereby the air over the wing breaks away from the top surface, causing the same loss of lift and vibration.

Just like worrying about my 5-year-old son scalding himself while he is attempting to make me a cup of coffee, we need to be able to prioritize the situation. My initial instincts aren't to worry about a potential stain on the carpet or a NAV ADR DISAGREE message as appeared in the Air France 447 flight deck. To enhance safety on board, the system needs to be able to evaluate the seriousness of what is taking place and to present only the vital information to the crew.

CHAPTER 5: EVOLUTIONARY ASPECTS OF THE BRAIN

The piloting of aircraft has evolved around the concept of a human brain being central to the operation. It started as a fun thing to do, and pleasure flights abounded to flood the human brain with dopamine as the individual underwent a completely new experience that human evolution had thrown away ages ago.

11/12. Darwinian Evolution, in its attempt to get airborne, could have given us wings but instead it gave us bats.

13. De Havilland DH.82 Tiger Moth cockpit (1930s)

So we designed and built flying machines with controls that could be interpreted by the human brain, and because we did not evolve with the necessary flying skills, we need to spend time teaching pilots how to adjust to the different environment, long ago mastered by the bats.

However, at all times when we are flying, we are interpreting the information via our neural network, the brain. We soon learnt that if we fly in cloud without the correct instrumentation and training, we will become disoriented and send the aircraft into a spiral dive, and so we exposed one of the several deficiencies of the airborne human brain.

Until we have finally cracked it and have invented the ultimate fully-independent automatic flight system, we need to work on integrating the human brain with the latest technology and should not be tempted to try to replace the brain in a rush to fulfill fantasies we find in the movies or fantasies we see in company accountant's profit projections. We shouldn't be taking undue risks. Although there are tolerances laid down on allowable percentages of failures in all sorts of industries, here, we should be aiming at zero tolerance. This seems to me to be how the human brain has evolved and survived to become the most intricate object in the entire universe. Each evolutionary step has to be managed very carefully so it doesn't prematurely extinguish the lineage but at the same time allowing greater plasticity within the new environment. Unless, of course, someone decides that it's acceptable from a statistical point of view to dabble in experiments for the greater good of mankind.

Nobody understands how the brain works, although present day computer systems, marketing and TV shows have seduced a lot of people into believing that the answer is just around the corner. This is all part of the impatience gene that needs to know the answer now! We have a long, long way to go.

Biological Neural Networks

In the quest to piece together an understanding of the synthesis of the human brain and computer technology, I have undertaken a bit of research on the make-up of the brain and reproduce it here to forward my argument — I don't profess to be an expert on the subject. The connection with computing and flight deck safety will come clear in a later chapter.

The human brain has over 100 billion neurons, called nerve cells or brain cells. Neurons communicate through thousands of individual connections to each other, which means that you have more connections in your brain than there are stars in the universe.

Every thought is a whole series of neurons communicating with each other and can be visualized as a network, like you may have a network of people who play tennis. No point in connecting with the golfer's network if you are hoping for Wimbledon tickets.

If we had a model of a brain just made of electrical wires and we switched on the current, then we would get total confusion and probably a massive short circuit. Eminent people who have gone before have discovered the mechanism that stops this: the synapse. This will only allow a connection if there is sufficient "weighting" to do so. When you learn to juggle with 3 balls, you will mostly drop some of them to start with; but as you practice, the neurons receive improved *weightings* as they more accurately estimate the requirements for a successful outcome, allowing you to eventually succeed, at least on to the next stage.

Messages move from neuron to neuron by chemicals called neurotransmitters across millionth-of-an-inch gaps called synapses. But they won't move across the synapse until that neuron has enough input energy (*weighting*) to make it happen. When learning to juggle, the neuron will have a score of 1 — no neurotransmitter is sent across and you drop the ball. But if you keep trying by practicing, the neuron gets higher and higher scores or weights until, say, score 5 — now a neurotransmitter is sent across and you catch the ball. The scoring system is achieved utilizing charged particles and use either charged sodium, potassium or chloride ions which move in and out of the cells and establish an electrical current. So if the cell has loads of positively charged particles then they induce the flow of electrons which are of course negatively charged particles.

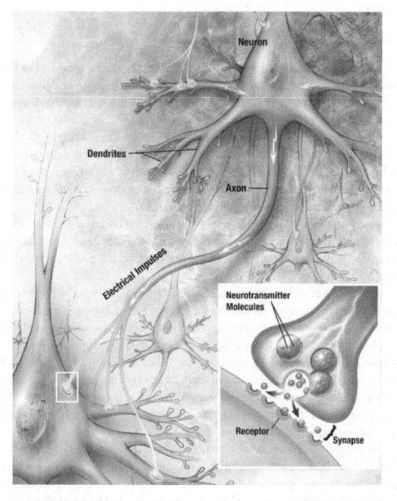

14. *Drawing illustrating the process of synaptic transmission in neurons*

Considering the "tennis" routing in the brain, we see above two neurons joined via a synapse which is indicated by the white box in the illustration. If I want some Wimbledon tickets, I need to get the name of the person that has access to tickets and for their name I need to connect with the neighboring neuron. Because this is important to me (there are also many other associated requests coming in from other neurons like excitement, emotion, friendship, etc.) the first neuron will "fire," facilitating the connection and I get the name.

The dendrites shown in the picture above are connections to other neurons. We have many circuits that can be used to find information and cross check other sections of the brain, like you would use to solve a cryptic crossword clue. The technical definition for "firing" is: *an action potential, or spike, causing neurotransmitters to be released across the synaptic cleft, causing an electrical signal in the postsynaptic neuron.*

15. Chemical synapse

When a signal comes from another neuron, the neurotransmitter chemical transmits across the synaptic gap and stimulates the little receptors on the other side. This opens what's called a Ligand gate which allows the ions (+ charged particles) to enter the cell and add to its overall electric charge. The cells start at -65 mv. As the ions enter the cell it increases a little to something like -63 mv but if other connections are also flooding in with signals, they all add up to what is the threshold value for an Action Potential or "firing." It now has so much positive charge that it registers at +40 mv. But soon after, the Ligand gates close and the system operates in reverse to restore the potential to -65 mv.

So the Action Potential is triggered which induces an electrical current to the next neuron. The axon (nerve) can go from your brain to your toe — quite a distance.

One problem for evolution was that the speed of transmission of the signal using the Ligand gates opening and closing was a bit slow and it looks like this branch of mammals died out by burning their toes in the hot thermal spring water, rendering them unable to run fast enough to hunt and feed themselves!

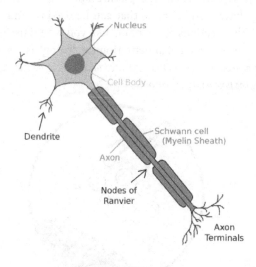

16. Diagram of a neuron showing Myelin Sheath

We were lucky, though, because another branch developed what we have now: fatty myelin, presumably because this branch of mammals lived in warmer climes and didn't have to use hot springs. Fatty myelin allows the positively charged particles to knock into one another, pushing the far right particle instantly out the other end. Electricity flows in the same way by each electron knocking into the next electron, meaning that the speed of electricity is perceived as practically instant and in fact travels at about 1/100 the speed of light (although the individual electrons are moving much more slowly).

Thoughts are derived from many sources (brain databases) and then voted upon (neuron Action Potentials) resulting in many routings or answers. The neuron system allows the entire database to be searched for compatibilities, and probably when we sleep the day's experiences are fed back into the brain, forming new connections. We can use the notion of it working in parallel because there are many answers/possibilities that take independent neural routes. It appears the system that actually handles and updates the connections is the key to our brain's success and that particular structured architecture is just not available today for our computers.

Furthermore, the brain can rearrange itself (for example, after someone has had a stroke), albeit not perfectly, and often with a huge amount of external input from professional trainers. To achieve this level of redundancy once a memory chip has burnt out would take some doing.

Computers don't have a deficiency due to inputs. They are not blind or senseless and nowadays can have more inputs than we have for our brains. If we see flames, feel heat, smell burning, taste smoke and hear a crackling sound; we have all the inputs we need to know that there is a fire. All these inputs can be provided to a computer to do the same thing, and we could even add a Geiger counter if we want, but the computer, like us, can still be fooled. If you showed the computer camera a high-definition film of a fire, would it tick the visual box? Would it then fire off the extinguisher? If not, how many ticked inputs do you need? We need more parallel neural analysis.

Another consideration, for successful symbiosis with computers, is a need to be able to process large data outputs from a computer which in turn can only be input to the human brain one by one. We need it further processed and presented to us in a singular, ordered format. If it displays multiple answers, we get confused by the enormity of the data, which was the problem the crew solved by putting in a Herculean effort on the Qantas 32 A380. The series computer can have multiple upstream failures that can't be digested so the discontinuities are designed to just spew out in an unintelligible way for the human brain to organize and interpret.

The brain has evolved many different ways of handling things in case something goes wrong. The computer has one way only — one accumulator (even if shared as in parallel computing discussed earlier). These extreme multiple outputs need to be rationalized and sorted so our "one bit of information at a time" brain can properly work together with the computer.

Artificial Neural Networks

An artificial neuron network is a computational model based on the structure and functions of biological neural networks. As has been mentioned, machine learning and artificial intelligence are being developed and can work well on a specific task, like face recognition or cancer diagnosis.

On the next page is the diagrammatical structure showing how input information is sorted by hidden layers that cross reference to each of the inputs before being sent to the output. The W in the diagram below stands for the *weighting* (probability of it being correct) of the values in the neuron connection. It also emulates our brain in that the hidden layers do all the work without us knowing. I will be using a simplified diagram based on this principle later.

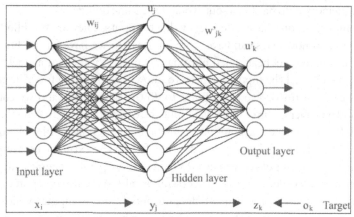

17. *Artificial Neural Networks diagram*

Series and Parallel

We have used these terms loosely so far to show differences between the human brain and the computer. The straightforward analogy is not too bad but we can further explore the comparison.

"A man stops his car in front of a hotel and immediately realizes he's just gone bankrupt. Why?" That's a riddle that was around a while ago and serves as a good example of the problem. Our brain finds it difficult to see the answer at first, and we learn from interacting with the questioner that this is a riddle. So we know we need to open up maximum neural pathways to solve the conundrum. We can demonstrate the fundamental process by using a more generalized diagram (as shown below) that is based on the artificial neuron network diagrams which are used to model artificial intelligence.

AI is attempting to mimic the human brain by working out how it comes to a conclusion based on a vast amount of data storage locations (neurons) that individually know nothing. The classic example is, how do we recognize a numeral, say 5? It could be typed in a clear font or written in practically illegible scrawl, but we somehow recognize the symbol. (Websites where you have to prove you are not a robot by matching a weirdly shaped symbol with a known keyboard character are pushing that notion to the limit!) By inserting examples of numbers into the Input Layer, the computer program works to the right through the hidden layers where refinements to the prob-ability are calculated. So if a 7 is inserted, it will assign a low probability that it is a 5, based on the structure of the pixels that make up the image.

The vertical component is attached to the left in the 5, and the right in the seven, so it's not looking good at this stage for the 7. There can be as many hidden layers as there are ways you can think of to discriminate between the numbers.

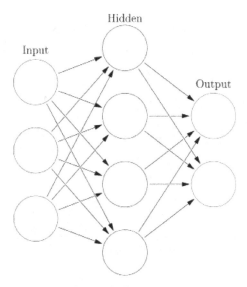

18. Simplified Artificial Neural Networks diagram

And the highest probability wins. The clever bit is what happens next — back propagation. The first run through the computer program will inevitably come up with a high level of inaccuracy, so there is a need to feedback the results into the system and run it again and again and again, all the time refining the probability that the character is a 5. All we have to do is calculate the new refinement weighting for each neuron.

But — there's a Catch 22 — this is impossible with the computing power we have today, it takes too long to do all the thousands of back calculations. So a shorthand or approximate calculation is used that doesn't take a month of Sundays to complete — which presumably is why face recognition is not as accurate as we would like it to be.

However, the principle is really interesting and I'm going to use, in a very approximate manner, the basic concept of the multiple connections and the weighting/probability to try and solve real-time problems, starting with the car/hotel riddle and eventually moving on to safety solutions in aviation.

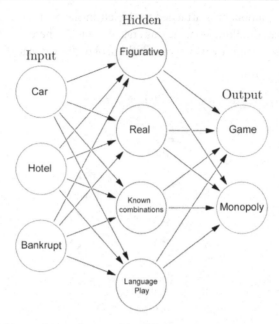

Simplified A.N.N. diagram for Monopoly riddle

From the diagram above, we have the 3 inputs on the left and examples of the hidden layers (thought processes) that enable us to come up with the solution. Interesting how we have the two expressions "come up with" and "work out." We need to find the connection, so we input Car, Hotel, and Bankrupt. Hidden to our consciousness, the neural pathways start to open up and multiple concepts are routed into the neurons. As it's a riddle, we know this may not be *real* and there may be *figurative* associations (that in itself being another neural network!). We may think of existing, *known combinations* where a car and a hotel are seen together. We may think there is some *language play* afoot here — Car, Hotel, Bankrupt. CHB or HCB or BCH? No, nothing there, so let's cut off the Action Potential in that section and continue searching.

I bet you have had the situation before, when you are trying to solve a riddle, remember a name or work out a crossword clue, and the next day, after a good sleep, the answer just pops into your head. Would that be the difference between "coming up with" the solution and "working out" the solution?

Soon the answer to our current puzzle reveals itself as the game "Monopoly." But not everyone will get it straightaway. This represents the parallel system of the human brain — it is sourcing multiple areas to solve the riddle. It is well documented that when people suddenly face death, their lives flash in front of them. They also report that time slows down. Could this be the neural network trying to find a solution to their predicament and running through the entire database for a solution, and at the same time removing needed energy from other bodily systems thus giving the appearance of time slowing?

19. Accumulator pinch point

How does the computer fare? As we have discussed before, the computer needs everything to go through the accumulator (even parallel computers have to share the calculations and coordinate).

The heart of a computer is the processor, where each line of code has to sequentially pass through the accumulator, which can be seen as a pinch point in the system. It will need to process Car, Hotel and Bankrupt one by one, but because it does this so quickly it gives the appearance of handling all 3 together at the same time. Much like the fast hands of a card trickster — it really does look like the Queen of Hearts is in the middle. Various possible connections are listed below in the table.

Car — Hotel	Hotel — Bankrupt	Car — Bankrupt
Door	Mortgage	Lease Company
Seat	Liquidator	Bank heist getaway car
Window	Bank	Liquidator
Motel	Monopoly game	
Parking		
Cost of Parking		
Caravan/RV		
Tired /Tired: Synonyms		

In the case of this puzzle, there are 6 possible combinations but [Car — Hotel] is the same as [Hotel — Car] so we are left with 3 combinations to compare. The programmer now has to come up with a method to cross-check the connections so they might program in these 3 lists of commonalities, some of which are stretching the limits of what could be referred to as a connection. Again, this is all greatly simplified for the sake of example:

The program is designed to find common entries, so firstly [Car — Hotel] is processed through the accumulator against [Car — Bankrupt].

FOR N = 1 TO ENDLIST
IF LIST (CAR — HOTEL) = LIST (CAR — BANKRUPT) THEN SAVE TO MEMORY
NEXT N

Nothing would be found here, so next, process [Car — Hotel] against [Hotel — Bankrupt]

FOR N = 1 TO ENDLIST
IF LIST (CAR — HOTEL) = LIST (HOTEL — BANKRUPT) THEN SAVE TO MEMORY
NEXT N

Nothing would be found here, so finally, process [Car — Bankrupt] against [Hotel — Bankrupt]

FOR N = 1 TO ENDLIST
IF LIST (CAR — BANKRUPT) = LIST (HOTEL — BANKRUPT) THEN SAVE TO MEMORY
NEXT N

This time we have a hit — "Liquidator" — the only problem is that it is the wrong answer. However, the programmer had very cleverly anticipated the actual answer by initially inserting one of the possibilities as Monopoly into the [Hotel — Bankrupt] list. But he should also have inserted Monopoly into the [Car — Bankrupt] list, although it is a slightly more tenuous link, in which case we would have got two answers. But how can we guarantee that any database is entirely complete? The computer can either give us the wrong answer or it could just dump out every entry on the lists, thus giving us the correct answer; but we would have an information overload trying to find it.

Now this is a very basic demonstration and you could easily think of other entries that could go into the lists, but it does indicate the crux of the matter. Unless you tell the computer what to look for, it hasn't got a clue. With machine learning, the computer can be told that it has been partially successful, so it can work towards greater accuracy; or a programmer can easily write extra code in an attempt to try and guess the answer for a particular problem. But until it can be wired up with neural pathways, it will struggle on the fully automated flight deck.

In the brain, the hidden pathways are actioned until the answer reveals itself, even if it takes all night. The series computer cannot access the same amount of material because there is no "sleep" system for updating the connections, and every eventuality has to be separately programmed in. Sleep, it appears, is the linchpin of our brain power — we must reorganize our filing system daily, that is why sleep is so necessary and why prolonged deprivation will lead to premature death. Could this be the evolutionary secret, perhaps, for our dominance in the world?

Horses for Courses

Here is a rudimentary table of the main pros and cons when considering computer vs. brain:

Computer Pros	Computer Cons	Brain Pros	Brain Cons
Very fast	Can only interpret a simple question	Huge Networking abilities	Rarely so fast
Very accurate in controlled circumstances	No by-pass, so vulnerable	Multiple by-pass	Runs out of energy
Never gets tired			Can't handle large amounts of data

Decision Making

The neural network makes our brains superior at complex decision making. Simple decisions we can do equally well as a computer. For instance, is 5 greater than 3 in a numerical context? Is 5,200,445,333.021 bigger than 5,200,445,333.001? But 5,200,445,333.021 divided by 13.21 would be no contest (although I'm led to believe there are some people that can actually do this!).

A complex decision needs a neural network. Flying into Islamabad in a 747-200 with classic old-fashioned round dials and limited computer-based navigation, we suffered a bad lightning strike on the underside of the starboard wing. It blew a 2 ft by 2 ft hole in the wing outer surface, which we didn't know about until we landed. But after the initial shock of the loud bang, the aircraft continued flying perfectly normally.

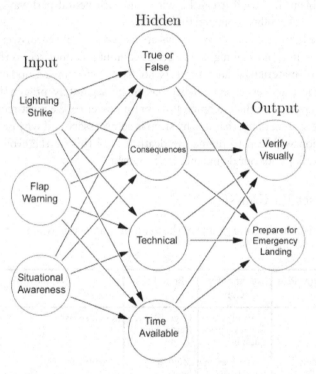

Simplified A.N.N. diagram for flap warning diagnosis

We were on the initial approach and selected the first stages of flap to position 5, which meant the leading edge high lift flaps should have been extended together with 5 degrees of flap from the rear of the wing. The problem was that we now had flap warning lights on in the flight deck suggesting that the leading and trailing edge flaps were not in position. The "simple decision" was to pull out the checklist and follow the documented procedure. In this case the checklist said that the flaps were stuck and we would have to set up the aircraft to land with limited flap, and therefore we would need to land about 50 kts faster, at about 210 mph. The "complex decision" was to look at all the other possibilities that could be leading us up the garden path within the time constraints of the remaining fuel.

This was our simplified neural diagram. Situation awareness refers to all the other operational aspects of flying the aircraft such as navigating safely in a mountainous area and flying a stable, unrushed approach. By using *technical* knowledge we reckoned that the lightning strike was unlikely to have jammed the flaps by a direct hit.

By considering the *consequences* of misdiagnosis, we realized that if we chose to land the aircraft at high speed with the flaps actually extended, the significant amount of extra lift could easily have resulted in us overrunning the end of the runway. By doubting what was in front of us and by pressing our faces against the rearmost flight deck windows, we could just see the wing tip leading edge flaps extended and appearing to be locked in position. We chose to ask the Flight Engineer to go back into the cabin for a visual inspection of the entire wing. All the flaps were out at the 5 degree mark and it was only the indication system that had got confused, presumably from the static charge of the lightning strike. We landed safely.

So our thought process can be visualized as multi-path neuron firing. The pseudo parallel, but series computer, can closely emulate the brain's parallel processing but for complex work it needs to have the answer pre-loaded and embedded somewhere within the database. We see this trick in our everyday search on-line using Google and similar search engines. It still amazes me how fast the search engine works and how it even throws up suggestions as to what I may be looking for before I've finished typing! It appears ridiculously intelligent; and then it comes back with not only the answer for me at the top of the page in about a millisecond but also a whole load of other possibilities. Because our brains are used to a relatively slow world, we are impressed by the speed of the answer; and provided we have asked a simple question, we know we are in the "sliced bread" area of invention. But what if we ask a complex question that requires the sort of problem solving we as a species have evolved as of primary importance over speed of response?

"Which is the best battery to buy?" will most likely give a list of the battery manufacturers that have paid the most for advertising. Way further down the list you may see a very good article on how all the major manufacturers compare and how they perform in different environments, which is actually what you want. The question is too complex for a present day computer, so it does what happens on a flight deck when all goes awry; it dumps out everything it knows at the time — for you to sort out. Just to emphasis the point here, some people argue that we are being tricked by search engines into thinking that their line-one answer is the only one that needs to be considered and as a result all sorts of abuses can occur when it comes to buying choices and political preferences. The truth can be distorted, and this is why I have used the word "trick" in describing the abilities of the computer — it is trying to make you believe it is working at your level — and therefore just as intelligent and aware.

This pseudo parallel trick is done by what are termed computer "interrupts." The hour-glass pinch point that processes the individual linear instructions and data, shares it's time with other functions. For instance, if you are working on a word-processor and an email comes along, your processor will very quickly pause your work, go and sort out the email (and ping you a notification symbol) before returning to see which keys you had pressed whilst it was otherwise occupied. There are many different types of interrupts these days, and eventually quite a queue builds. In days gone by, if too many inputs came along at the same time, you may even have been visited by the dreaded "blue screen of death"!

One day we will get there but for now and for the continued safety of our passengers and crew we need to work as closely as we can with our own neural networks and our current computers. We need to recognize both of our limitations and then extract the best from each system. Computers have been a huge benefit in the evolution of the flight deck, saving many lives and taking pressure off the pilot, which in turn leaves her time and space to monitor for other dangers, especially in the takeoff and landing phase of flight. But we need to accept that if we are to further improve safety, not just in aviation, I might add, we need to work on these integrated systems. A good analogy might be that of a House of Cards.

ID 79369779 © Hannu Viitanen | Dream-stime.com

Computers assist us and enhance flight deck safety up to a certain point, which is visualized here as 4 layers of cards. If we try to build a 5th layer, vulnerabilities creep in. It then becomes too complicated and very hard to interface with our human perceptions. Are the flaps out or not? This would have been a 5th layer question for the computer and too difficult to program.

ID 79369779 © Hannu Viitanen | Dream-stime.com

However good all the individual components, the entire concept/system can come crashing down if one of the areas (cards) becomes displaced. Air France 447 lost just one card (icing of the pitot probes) and as there was no joint integrated system designed in, the human system diverged with the computer system.

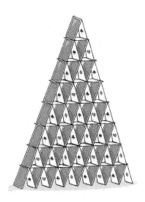

ID 35861599 © Igor Zakowski | Dream-stime.com

We could add extra layers of safety by installing backup systems on top of backup systems. For instance, there could be a backup ice detector on the pitot tube which would automatically switch in a separate source of heating. We could have independent flap position detectors all over the wing in case the primary system fell foul of a lightning strike. But if we continue adding monitoring software into the series type computer systems, we make the entire system potentially more vulnerable as now there are more areas (cards) which can fail but one deficiency could still bring the whole thing down.

A properly integrated system would look like this:

Human brain *Series Computer* *Integration System*

If the Swiss cheese started to line up in a difficult situation, with an integration system we might be able to recover without fatalities.

Human Fail *Computer Fail* *Integration Survive*

All House of Card images courtesy of Dreamstime.

CHAPTER 6: INTEGRATION

The fascinating trick of biological evolution is that once it has started out on an idea, it seems to somehow successfully carry this forward without yet having had the opportunity to take on any benefits from the original random mutation, and at the same time without throwing out the baby with the bathwater and terminating that specific evolutionary line. An example would be the brain's neural network undergoing a random evolutionary step to develop synapses and then to somehow produce fast-relaying fatty myelin to further improve the system.

We have the advantage of being able to apply some sort of reasoning to the further improvement of our development, as we do with genetically modified crops and cloning animals like Dolly the sheep from a single adult cell. Behavioral Computer Science will be the discipline at the forefront of our evolution towards fully automatic airliners, and it will need to emulate the most successful strategies of evolution. Computers do a brilliant job carrying out repeated actions on limited tasks at high speed and with high accuracy. Humans do a brilliant job carrying out limited actions on vast array of very complex tasks. One day computers may replace the human brain, probably by synthesizing a neural network, but until then if we are to further improve what is already an extremely high safety standard, I would suggest we need to coordinate what we have evolved so far.

Introducing the next generation Artificial Neural Networks and Multi-layer Perception will be the equivalent of adding another layer onto the house of cards, programmed into our present-day systems. Possibly, we need to pause, and take a parallel step to better co-ordinate both systems for maximum effect in support of pilots (and potentially many other computer-dependent sectors) through the transition period.

The computer house of cards can be built only so high, as could be deduced from the safety statistics for 2018. If we can set up integrated monitoring systems working together with the series computers we have today, it should have maximum effect on the improvement of safety statistics. Humans and computers need to be partnered such that when a serious situation develops (unavoidable Swiss cheese), the three systems will work together, backing each other up with the aim of presenting the human pilot with the perfect information at the critical time in the clearest format.

So far, we have made a brief digression into our brain's make up and how well the microprocessor interacts with our world. We have observed how both pilots and series computers can fail catastrophically; so now we're off to consider an alternative path of evolution which may produce a more balanced symbiosis between man and machine. One solution may be to awaken the "2001 monolith" and contrive the rebirth of HAL.

20. *HAL — Heuristically Programmed ALgorithmic Computer*

Known as the Heuristically Programmed ALgorithmic Computer, the system was designed to run the entire *2001* "Discovery One" spacecraft en route to Mars. Heuristic means "enabling people to discover or learn something for themselves" — so what we effectively have in the movie is the Holy Grail of a fully functioning Artificially Intelligent computer.

More accurately HAL was a HAL 9000, which suggests that the creation was the end result of a long development program, and it apparently was built in Illinois as production number 3. Stanley Kubrick and Arthur C. Clarke imagined many jumps of technological advance to get HAL up to the standard depicted, and somehow they got through the present day barrier that has led to a stubborn resistance to the expected decline of commercial aircraft accidents.

How unrealistic is this notion of an omnipresent computer system monitoring the flight deck? Let's put aside the technological problems it poses
for the moment and look firstly at what advantages it might offer us. HAL
primarily perceived the human environment through a camera and would
have observed, quite independently, that the flaps weren't selected "down"
on Spanair Flight 5022, regardless of the temperature sensor status and
circuit breaker position. It would integrate with our world and interpret it
acting as a separate, independent house of cards. So in line with our discus
far, we would have the following picture:

Pilots   *Series Computer*   *HAL System*

- The first house of cards represents the human pilot pair that we
have today on a modern flight deck, which works extremely well.
The acceptable pilot workload tolerance is represented by 4 layers of
cards. A fifth layer could compromise safety by increasing the workload, leading to cognitive overload.
- The second house of cards represents the customary array of CRT/
LCD displays and series computers which we have on the flight deck
today. The acceptable computer dependence is represented by 4
layers of cards. A fifth layer could compromise safety by over reliance
on the computer's ability to recognize real world problems.
- The third house of cards is the HAL system which will run independently of the series style computers to fill in the gaps or cheese holes.
It will include an independent GPS and Independent Trip Counter
with Performance and other databases. The system, once established,
could even be able to learn during its life (using backpropagation and
deep learning) so it could perform to an ever-increasing higher level of
proficiency. The HAL computer dependence is again represented by 4
layers of cards. A fifth layer could compromise safety due to over reliance on HAL's ability to recognize real world problems. The essential
element of this third house of cards is that it will offer assistance to
the operation to prevent it from becoming super-critical

HAL would act like a good heavy pilot that we mentioned in a previous chapter. The "Heavy" is the extra pilot that is only required for in-flight rest purposes but that offers what can be vital input, by observing the overall operation of the aircraft, especially during the takeoff and landing phases. The extra crew that were involved with the Qantas A380 flight departing Singapore, where an engine explosion damaged the wing and caused multiple warnings on the flight deck, greatly assisted the operating crew with the decision making and logic handling. Effectively, we need HAL to be a "phantom" heavy pilot, discretely but overtly pointing out any deficiencies on the flight deck and at the same time knowing when not to bring up something trivial that could be a distraction.

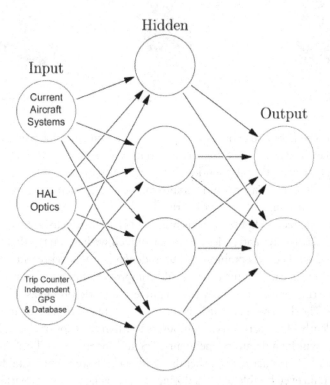

So maybe rather than "Heuristically Programmed ALgorithmic Computer," a better name for our HAL system would be "Heavy Aircrew Logic" or "Heavy Assisted Logic" in consideration of other fields that could benefit from this concept of "computer–human" symbiosis. From here on, I will refer to the new system as HAL.

Earlier, we introduced a more generalized diagram that is based on the artificial neuron network diagrams used to model Artificial Intelligence. Although at present the HAL system is not predicated on AI, the diagrams are quite useful in demonstrating the cross connections and offer a good diagrammatic representation of the logic behind the HAL concept. This (above) would be our neural network, or HAL diagram, illustrating how each system is connected and backed up. There will be various hidden elements which will sort the chaff from the wheat and finally the output, according to the criticality of the event, is presented to the pilots.

There are 3 main inputs: human pilots, series computers and HAL. The human pilots overlook the entire system, receiving information from flight instruments and HAL, so there is no need to include them in the diagrams — they receive information from the right hand side "output" column.

Series computers are represented by the "Current Aircraft Systems." This refers to the primary sources of display to the pilots that is utilized today; we would still be using a standard operation but now with greater independent review. The majority of airliner flight decks around the world are either Boeing or Airbus and are very similar. This does, though, introduce another two significant advantages of HAL which we will pick up on later.

HAL Optics refers to the visual component of HAL that will take in data from the flight deck. Independent GPS (Global Positioning System) refers to what we are all currently familiar with in our smart phones, and *Trip Counter & Database* is the final part of HAL which includes performance data, terrain data and more. Performance data refers to the calculations that are required to ensure an aircraft can safely get airborne from a particular runway at a given takeoff weight. The trip counter is needed to work out which phase of flight the aircraft is currently experiencing. This way, if the flaps were up when the aircraft was on the gate, it wouldn't issue an alert; but if the aircraft was about to take off with the flaps up, then an alert would be issued. All flight instruments, Primary Flight Displays (PFD), Navigation Display (ND) and EICAS (Engine Indication and Crew Alerting System) would be monitored by HAL.

If this all seems a tad over-ambitious, let me mention that the technology required for this can easily be handled by one of today's smart phones; later I will show how I have built a demonstration HAL program running on a smart phone, working in association with a simulator display. Note to pilots: nothing would be recorded as in "video camera mode," since history tells us that recording it would only reduce safety. Humans get nervous about being spied upon — this would be a live, in the moment, alerting system based upon optimum response and interaction from a "phantom" Heavy pilot.

Let's look at an example of a HAL diagram for the Spanair 5022 situation. It happened to be the MD-82, but the diagrams don't have to be specific to the actual aircraft involved as they act as a universal example of the flap handling logic. After that, the stall-handling logic example follows, which was relevant to Air France 447.

Flap Handling Logic

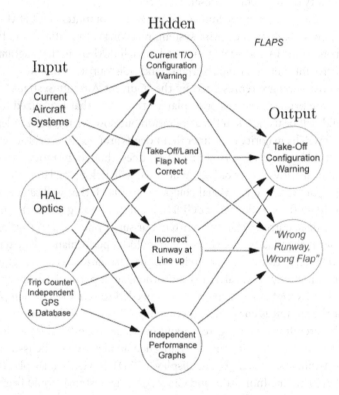

Spanair Flight 5022 was a scheduled domestic passenger flight from Barcelona–El Prat Airport to Gran Canaria Airport, via Madrid–Barajas. It crashed just after takeoff from runway 36L on August 20, 2008. The aircraft started the takeoff roll without the necessary flaps/slats (high lift devices) selected. This was a result of the aircraft having returned to stand to fix a temperature sensor overheat. Unfortunately, the fix involved shutting down the circuit for the temperature sensor (pulling a circuit breaker) which was in series with the Takeoff warning system. As a result, now being late, a human error crept in whereby they forgot to lower the flaps for takeoff and there was no warning system available. The aircraft crashed as it attempted to get airborne with insufficient lift — with 154 casualties.

The safety layers together with our new HAL system would be these:

- Throttle open with flaps out of range (currently in use)
- Optics detect flap position not as flight Manual demands
- Trip Counter detects T/O phase and reviews independent Performance Database against HAL GPS to ensure correct Takeoff runway
- Runway heading cross-checked against power setting plus HAL GPS ensures correct Takeoff runway even if flap setting is correct.

All 4 of these systems could independently raise an alert. Possible HAL Outputs — "WRONG FLAP, WRONG RUNWAY"

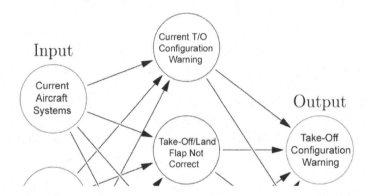

The top pathways are what are currently in place. The FMC/MCDU stores the required T/O flap setting. Hidden to the pilots is a safety system that raises a takeoff configuration alert if the pilots open the thrust levers beyond a specific point on the throttle quadrant with the flaps out of takeoff range.

The mid pathway HAL optics detect that the pilots have selected Flap 10 — the system knows from its database that Flap 20 is the minimum required. The lower pathway Trip Counter detects that the plane is taxiing and very close to the takeoff runway, which results in an independent HAL takeoff configuration alert.

On a separate occasion, the bottom pathway HAL optics detect the pilots have selected Flap 20 correctly but its database has calculated that

Flap 20 is still insufficient because the actual runway being used is incorrect. An independent "Wrong Runway" alert is issued. This could occur if the aircraft was accidentally about to take off on the wrong parallel runway in low visibility conditions.

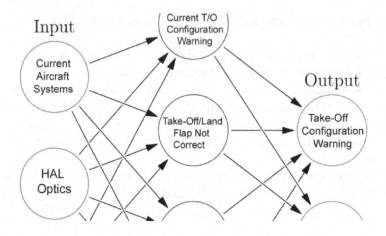

On a further separate occasion, using the bottom pathway, the HAL optics detect that the aircraft heading is not aligned with the selected takeoff runway, with 3/4 power set, and issues a "Wrong Runway" alert. Again this could occur if the aircraft was accidentally about to take off from the wrong runway at an airfield where two runways go in different directions but share a common threshold area, a situation that GPS alone could not detect.

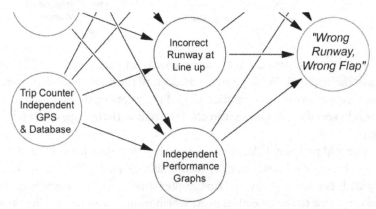

The first and only layer of system backup was fallible for Spanair 5022 because the circuit breaker had been tripped. HAL would provide independent monitoring to catch the error. Is there an argument that this could be overdoing it somewhat, as it appears to be a very rare occurrence?

Spanair 5022 crashed on August 20, 2008. On August 16, 1987, the exact same thing happened to Northwest Airlines Flight 255 at Detroit-Metro airport. The aircraft had not returned to stand with a technical fault and so the series Takeoff Configuration alert was active — or was it? It appears that for some reason there was no power to the system and the inquiry concludes:

- The circuit breaker was intentionally opened by either the flight crew or maintenance personnel.
- The circuit breaker tripped because of a transient overload and the flight crew did not detect the open circuit breaker.
- The circuit breaker did not allow current to flow to the CAWS power supply and did not annunciate the condition by tripping.

These situations will sadly keep happening. Could a virtual heavy pilot monitoring the operation be a solution for not only this set of particular circumstances but countless others?

Air France 447 was at cruising altitude, flying through an area of dense thunderstorms over the South Atlantic Ocean. A pitot tube froze over and thus false data was fed into the computer. The pitot tube system comprises forward-facing probes to detect the force of air particles entering the tubes and thus it provides airspeed indication. Without the airspeed data, the crew became disorientated and may have thought that they were in an overspeed situation if the Air Data Computers were presenting false readings. Even if they had followed the Standby Airspeed Indicator (a spare mechanical instrument to act as an arbiter if the two main systems fail), when airspeed tubes get blocked and the aircraft climbs, the static pressure reduction drives the airspeed indicator to falsely indicate increased speed. So the natural tendency is to reduce the power and pull up the nose to reduce speed, which in turn further reduces the pressure and indicates more of a false overspeed. The aircraft low-speed stalled all the way down to the ocean.

Stall Handling Logic

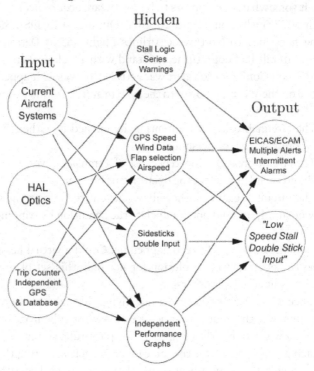

The safety layers with the new HAL monitoring system would be these:

- Multiple warnings with intermittent alarms (currently in use).
- Trip Counter & Database inputs note GPS ground speed.
- Trip Counter detects CRUISE phase and that flaps-up speed should be higher than current GPS speed ± wind.
- Optics see flap position is correct for cruise but senses double side-stick input

All 4 of these systems could independently raise an alert.

Outputs — "LOW SPEED, DOUBLE STICK INPUT"
"GPS CURRENTLY 180 KTS, GPS REQUIRES 250–340 KTS"

The captain had to work out what was going on, having come back to the flight deck from his rest. He was taking his rest so he would be able to safely operate the aircraft during the more critical descent and landing phase much later on. This is what the computer was telling him, according to the accident report:

> The ECAM system (Crew alert display) detected airspeed errors and so gave out a set of serial warnings. NAV ADR DISAGREE indi-cated that there was a disagreement between the three independent air data systems and a fault message for the flight management guid-ance and envelope computer was sent. One of the two final messages transmitted was a warning referring to the air data reference system, the other ADVISORY was a "cabin vertical speed warning."

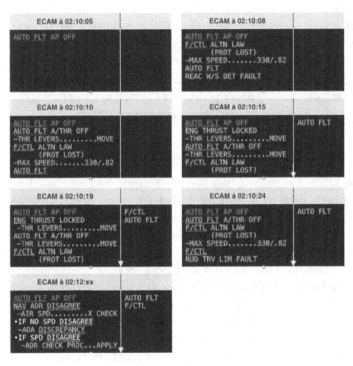

21. ECAM warnings — Air France 447

These were the ECAM warnings, over time, confronting the captain with additional alarms sounding intermittently to add to the confusion.

All he needed was a simple clue — "LOW SPEED, DOUBLE STICK INPUT."

Another benefit of this monitoring system comes in the Crew Resource Management arena. For those not familiar, the idea is to positively encourage all crew to work as a team and specifically to stay in "adult" mode when working together and not to set up a competitive atmosphere within the flight deck. This too is important in the wider aviation environment to enhance safety under the heading of "human factors."

In order to operate as a commercial pilot these days, one has to have attended one of the Crew Resource Management courses. The aviation world started realizing this a few years ago and designed CRM courses to improve flight crew communications between captain and first officer, which previously had resulted in not only several accidents but arguably the worst ever aviation accident, which took place in the Canaries when two 747s collided on the runway.

Now, if a crew received a "WRONG FLAP, WRONG RUNWAY" warning from HAL, it would register to both crew that they together had made a mistake, not just the one individual who hadn't picked up on the flap error. Before CRM, that individual who made the mistake and is now under duress was far more likely to under-perform at a critical moment during the subsequent flight. HAL therefore would act as a neutral arbiter.

Accident Types in Order of Frequency

Aviation safety has evolved to a very high degree and we should be mindful that in the drive to improve the statistics, it would be dangerous to change anything radically. The aim is to make improvements by analyzing past accidents and building a system that picks up at the critical point where current systems have proved vulnerable.

The table below lists the statistics for serious incidents and fatal accidents over the last 10 years (2010–2019). This is a good representation of what is still slipping through the net despite an amazing effort within the industry for zero tolerance. About half of these accidents may be able to be avoided in future if a HAL system were introduced. There were about 109 serious incidents involving fatalities of which 58 could not be assisted by enhanced monitoring systems, for example a bomb or an errant firing of a surface to air missile. However, it should help with other failures by assisting the crew with essential "need to know" information that can be easily overlooked in the confusion of an emergency.

There have also been many "too close for comfort" incidents that the system will take out of the mix. For instance, other that the two previously discussed accidents, a few aircraft have started the takeoff roll without any flap being selected and have luckily got airborne without incident. Maybe this is great flying skill by the pilots or inherent good design of the aircraft but it would be preferable to have the chance element removed.

HAL Assist	No.	Type of Accident
NAVIGATION (APPROACH 27) (TERRAIN 19)	46	Navigational Error
R/W EXCURSION	24	Runway Excursion
ENGINE FAILURE	19	Engine Failure
FIRE	10	External Fire
WEATHER	7	Microburst or Windshear related
INSTRUMENT	6	Instrumentation fault
ICING	6	Not de-iced/Iced up
VERTIGO G/A & T/O	6	Go-Around then somatogravic illusion
SUICIDE	5	Suicide
DOUBLE ENGINE FAILURE	4	Double Engine Failure
SLOW G/A	4	On Approach with late Go-Around
G/A STALL	2	Stall
FUEL	2	Insufficient Fuel, Fuel leak
FLAP	1	Wrong Flap
Unavoidable		
TECHNICAL	6	Technical fault on aircraft or Pilot error
TRIM	6	Loadsheet/Loading problem
HIJACK	5	Hijack
BOMB	3	Terrorist attack
PERFORMANCE	1	Takeoff Performance
ATC	1	ATC error

Of these accidents, 31 out of 164 (19%) involved long haul aircraft which traditionally attract more senior and experienced pilots. About 40% of all airliners are long haul so if it was an even spread you would expect 66 of these accidents to be on long haul aircraft. In which case you might conclude that long haul crews are safer due to their experience. However, short haul aircraft carry out about 3 times as many takeoffs and landings so if 60% of aircraft are short haul, this would amount to 98 (60% x 164) short haul flights. If we now triple this to take account of the extra takeoff and landings, we arrive at a figure of 3 x 98 = 294 flights. The amount of short haul incidents was 131 (80%) so 131 out of 294 flights = 45% which is less than half. So there seems to be no real difference between long haul and short haul pilots and the associated experience levels.

It's very difficult to work out whether experience makes an overall difference. A long haul pilot has to deal with fatigue moreso than a short haul pilot and also gets less hands-on practice. A lot of long haul flights have the "Heavy" extra crew member we have spoken about to help with the en-route rest. So long haul vs. short haul doesn't come into the argument, long and short haul pilots need every assistance they can get when things go wrong.

We will examine each of these categories of accidents using the HAL diagram and a working example from my Android Application monitoring a simulator display. These HAL diagrams illustrate the basic structure of the network but there would be no limitation to the number of hidden elements of the program. What's important is that each hidden element of the network works independently feeding in data to a relatively simple central decision making interpreter to raise an alert. The pilots would need relatively little extra training and would consider the system to be the equivalent of an extra pilot onboard who is solely there to assist.

A little more about the Optics. The placement of these cameras will be discussed later but essentially they will read existing data off the PFD — ND — EICAS/ECAM screens (current aircraft systems) and independently process the flight status. Another camera/detector will be constantly monitoring how many persons are present on the flight deck at any one time with the door locked. The reason for this will become clear later. The Independent Trip Counter, an integral part of HAL, will take in several cues and sense the phase of flight. Any internal failings of HAL would be indicated on the HAL "Interface Serviceability Indicator" adjacent to the PFD so the crew will know if they are down to 2 pilots again!

So what information do we need to feed HAL? We need specific inputs from the Primary Flight Display (PFD), the Navigation Display (ND) and the Engine-Indicating and Crew-Alerting System (EICAS) or ECAM on Airbus. We also need to link in the flight deck personnel detector and as a further enhancement, there is the availability to link in specialized external detectors.

Flight Displays

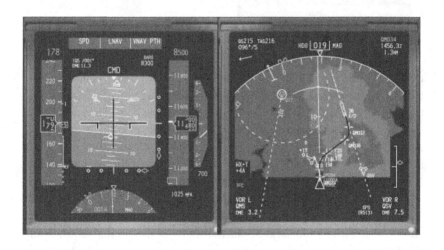

22. Primary Flight Display and Navigation Display

The Primary Flight Display (above left), or similar style of presentation, is the main instrument used by pilots to control the flight path of the aircraft. The central section shows the aircraft in a left turn and pitched up at about 6 degrees. The tape to the left shows speed, the tape to the right displays altitude. The arc at the bottom indicates the direction that the aircraft is flying (heading). The two crossed bars in the middle (the Flight Director) move to show the pilot how she should be flying to ensure the aircraft follows the correct course. The display is also color coded so any parameters of the same color as the Flight Director depict a target that the pilot should be aiming towards, whether it be a speed, an altitude or a heading. There is also much other data that is presented on the Primary Flight Display.

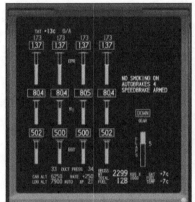 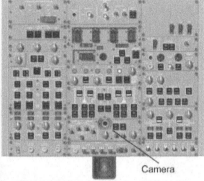

23/24. EICAS and Overhead panel indicating camera placement

The Navigation Display (above right), or similar style of presentation, is the main instrument used by pilots to navigate the aircraft. The little white triangle at the bottom is a depiction of the aircraft on the map. The arc at the top shows the direction that the aircraft is flying (heading). The line leading from the white triangle to the runway indicates the intended track of the aircraft. The arrow at top left, and readout above, displays the current wind direction and speed. There is also much other data that is presented on the Navigation Display.

The Engine-Indicating and Crew-Alerting System (EICAS) or ECAM on Airbus, is the main instrument used by pilots to set engine power and to receive any warning messages about the status of the aircraft (above left). The little white boxes contain the relevant engine parameters of EPR (Engine Pressure Ratio or Thrust), N1 (Revolutions per minute of the engine) and EGT (Exhaust Gas Temperature or engine temperature). There is also much other data that is presented on the EICAS display.

A People/Person detector would sense how many persons are on the flight deck with the door locked at any one time. This will be a separate camera/detector positioned to be able to scan the entire flight deck area (as indicated on the overhead panel, above right).

Trialling HAL in a Smart Phone

Earlier, we put aside the technological problems posed by HAL and looked at two fatal accidents that would almost certainly have benefited from the system. Now we can look at how Heavy Aircrew Logic can be demonstrated in the form of an Android Application running on a smart phone which in turn is reading data off a remote, unconnected computer running a flight simulator.

I have taken examples from fatal accidents that have occurred in the last 10 years (2010–2019) and for which HAL could have made a significant contribution to avert the accident altogether. There are many more combinations and permutations of crosschecking elements that can be inserted into the hidden logic to provide further layers of protection and is only restricted by the limitations of our "parallel" brains.

The smart phone setup follows the same principle with our 3 layers of:

PILOTS — SERIES COMPUTERS — HAL SYSTEM

The pilots will be receiving prompts from the smart phone running the HAL software. The simulator provides the regular flight deck displays and is considered as the series computer. The HAL smart phone will be interpreting the simulator and offering options to the pilots when applicable.

The simulator is based on the 747- 400 and for simplicity is a hybrid of the main flight displays on the flight deck as below. Note the sidestick has been added (bottom left) in consideration of the Airbus configuration. The simulator displays the relevant data that will be real-time scanned and read by HAL to provide the input for its own independent calculations and pre-programmed awareness of the pilot/aircraft situation.

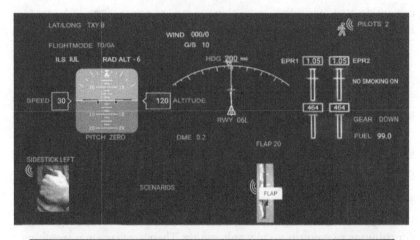

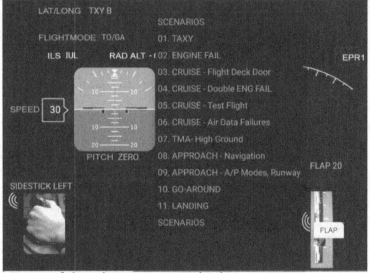

25. *Generic flight simulator running on a Windows laptop*

26. *Scenarios taken from the last 10 years of accidents (2010–2019)*

Ten scenarios have been programmed, with an extra one named "Test Flight" where the simulator is flying around at 25,000 ft, allowing the user to interact with the flight deck to test HAL's ability in different flight phases and, importantly, with varying unexpected combinations. A mouse click on various sections will change the configuration, like flap up or down, power increase or decrease etc.

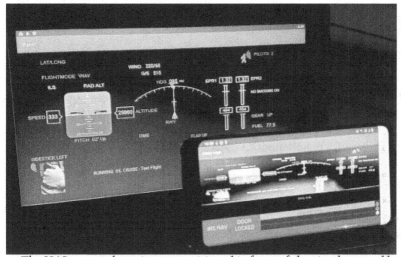

The HAL smart phone is now positioned in front of the simulator and by clicking on one of the scenarios (1 to 11 above) the flight sequence plays out on the simulator while HAL monitors and reacts.

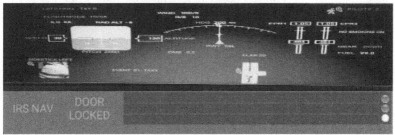

27. HAL smartphone monitors and reacts to the simulator

28. Heavy Aircrew Logic provides backup for the flight crew

This is the HAL application (above) with the top half of the screen showing the simulator data seen by the camera. It is somewhat distorted but this is just the way the wide angle camera presents the image. The display is only there for demonstration purposes and it is not necessary for the system to function, as the data is extracted in the software. The IRS NAV and DOOR LOCKED messages are also only displayed as part of the simulation process and would not be visible to the pilots. The lower part of the screen is the only visible interface between HAL and the crew with voice and discrete chimes enhancing the system.

The actual HAL interface, shown above, would consist of 3 LED bars and a Serviceability Indicator on the right. There would be two positioned on the flight deck, one on each side for captain and first officer and most likely placed near the Primary Flight Display (PFD) where it can be clearly seen. An applicable chime sounds to announce a message.

So, already you might be thinking, "What happens if the view is blocked"? The rationale is again linked to the Heavy pilot concept. Currently, if the two operating pilots actively want to degrade the safety of the operation then they can ask the Heavy pilot to leave the flight deck which would be the same as putting your hand over the camera lens.

These would be the functions of the Serviceability Indicator:

 Normal operations. Pilots can rely on critical feedback from HAL (green light).

 Camera covered and unable to detect anything. This would be the equivalent of removing the Heavy pilot off the flight deck and therefore purposely degrading the safety of the aircraft. It would also be a system fail/Off indication (red light).

 Specific data has been blocked on the PFD. This could be by accident if blocking a section of the PFD or ND with a hand or checklist, e.g., the speed readout. It acts as a reminder to restore camera access. HAL can differentiate between a blockage and missing data from the PFD/ND due to a fault or shutdown (amber and green lights).

The third line on the HAL interface is used to provide a warning message from the Serviceability Indicator which will remain lit until the situation reverts. The text won't appear if there is a more urgent message utilizing the third line but the Serviceability Indicator still reacts accordingly.

GEAR IS DOWN

The color coding is in line with the accepted philosophy, red for warning and amber for alert. As an example, the warning above (red) would appear when the gear has been mistakenly left down after a go-around. HAL would override this alert if there was a non-normal situation involving the gear.

Navigational Error During Approach (27 fatal accidents 2010–2019)

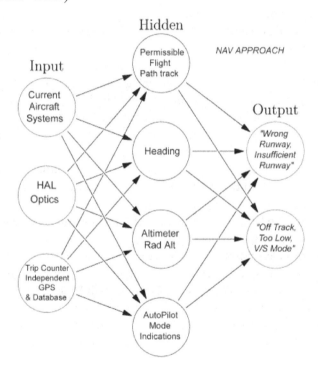

The next section offers examples of how HAL would have provided the necessary alerts to avoid about half of the accidents that involved fatalities over the past 10 years (2010 — 2019). We start with the most frequent type of accident and working down the list to the least frequent. Each scenario has a HAL (Heavy Aircrew Logic) diagram and a description of how it works in real time using the Android application monitoring the simulator. Each of the HAL interface images are screenshots of the working application captured during the simulation, providing the relevant information to both pilots at the most appropriate time.

- Hidden logic — lateral and horizontal acceptable final approach flight path tolerances are programmed internally and HAL tracks the descent with independent GPS and altimeter readouts.
- Once the aircraft transits out of the safe approach path area (trip lines), either vertically or laterally, graded warnings are activated. An escape route is suggested following the published go-around routing if possible.
- Autopilot Modes checked and warnings activated. For example, V/S Mode (Vertical Speed) selected while too low on approach with autopilot engaged.

Independent worldwide data containing information on high ground and lowest permissible altitude to fly is incorporated into the HAL database, but when the aircraft gets close to the airport it needs to descend below the area safety heights in order to land. This is where it becomes a little trickier in safeguarding the approach phase with current systems.

Here, Kathmandu is a good example of a challenging airfield. See below for the Approach Chart that pilots typically use for guidance around the high ground. The airport's runway is depicted at top right of the chart and the inbound course to land is 022 degrees, so the final inbound course is flown from the South, heading roughly up the page.

The HAL independent GPS will detect if the aircraft is ever laterally displaced by more than a permissible distance from any high ground in which case a warning will be issued. The same will happen with the final descent phase or what pilots refer to as the vertical profile. Note the excerpt below from the approach chart (figure 30). This tells the pilots the lowest possible heights to fly when at certain distances from the airport.

Example 1, Kathmandu — Chart Information

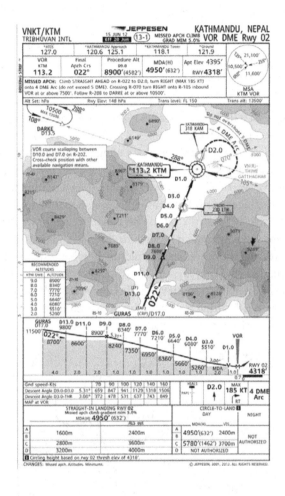

29. *Jeppesen approach chart for Kathmandu, Nepal.*
Reproduced with permission of Jeppesen Sanderson, Inc.
NOT FOR NAVIGATIONAL USE

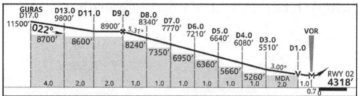

30. *Jeppesen descent profile for Kathmandu, Nepal*

For example, at a distance of 9 miles (D9.0) from the Kathmandu beacon (113.2 KTM) the aircraft should be at 8,900 ft. Any lower and you risk hitting the high ground, any higher and you risk having to dive down too steeply to get to the runway for a safe landing. HAL's independent GPS will detect if the aircraft is ever vertically displaced by more than a permissible distance where it will impinge a Trip Line, in which case a warning will be issued. In fact, this is exactly what the pilot who is not actually flying the aircraft should be doing anyway, calling out any deviations and assisting the other pilot by re-enforcing the overall mental picture of what is happening around them — bearing in mind they are very likely to be in cloud. HAL's sensitivity will be such that it will only intervene if dangerously off course. The last thing the pilots need during a demanding approach is the distraction of a nagging, over sensitive intervention adding to the workload.

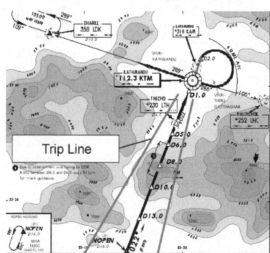

Reproduced with permission of Jeppesen Sanderson, Inc.

NOT FOR NAVIGATIONAL USE

But if it all goes wrong, HAL will interject with a reminder to keep them on course and away from high ground. If the system detects that on short finals the aircraft is too far from the runway and seconds from undershooting into the ground, a more forceful reminder will be issued via voice message.

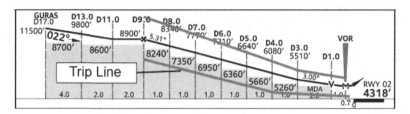

31. Warning given if Trip lines are breached either vertically or laterally

Most aircraft these days have databases that are linked to the autopilot navigation systems so the pilots can load up the Kathmandu VOR/DME approach for runway 02. But the pilots on some older aircraft may still have to make altitude selections all the way down the approach which is where errors can creep in, especially in bad weather. Crucially, HAL will back up the pilots whether the approach is fully automatic in a modern aircraft or semi-automatic in an older aircraft.

Simulation 1 — Kathmandu

The simulation starts 10 miles from touchdown at Kathmandu on a VOR/DME approach to runway 02. The aircraft is being flown with the autopilot engaged but not linked into the aircraft's navigation database. They are at 8,900 ft on track inbound to the runway and awaiting the 9.0 DME point where they will further descend at a constant rate until the runway becomes visual. Here, though, our crew is distracted and they fly past the descent point at 9 miles. HAL knows they are executing a VOR/DME approach by scanning the PFD and ND to ascertain which beacons and which runway have been selected.

At 7.4 miles HAL warns they are now high on the approach. This would have been preceded by a gentle nudge but has been omitted here.

The crew decide to Go-Around which HAL senses from monitoring the flight instruments and provides sequenced instructions to follow the published missed approach procedure.

By looking straight ahead at the HAL interface, the crew minimizes risk of somatogravic illusion or vertigo.

Using wind readout and GPS, HAL continues with correction guidance to maintain the published missed approach procedure.

This is just one scenario of many that could occur on this approach into Kathmandu. HAL is programmed to spot many different combinations at any airport where things have historically gone very wrong.

Los Angeles is a good example of a busy airfield with two pairs of very close parallel runways, one pair to the north and the other to the south. The Approach Chart that pilots typically use for guidance into Los Angeles for runway 24 Right is shown on the facing page. The airport's runway is depicted at middle left of the plate and the inbound course to land is 251 degrees, towards the coastline from the east. The independent GPS will detect if the aircraft is ever laterally or vertically displaced by more than a permissible distance in which case a warning will be issued.

A LOC or localizer approach is offered by ATC when the vertical guidance element (glide slope) of the ILS (Instrument Landing System) is unserviceable. Normally an autopilot can latch onto both the lateral and vertical guidance beams radiating from the runway and fly the aircraft right down to the landing. However it can't do this on a LOC approach — the pilots must control the correct descent profile if not able to use the aircraft's navigation database (RNAV approach).

Example 2, Los Angeles — Chart information

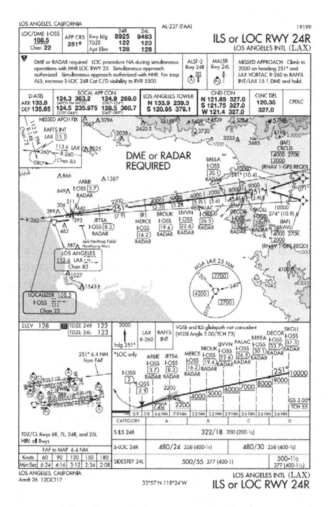

32. Jeppesen approach chart for Los Angeles, USA. Reproduced with permission of Jeppesen Sanderson, Inc.

NOT FOR NAVIGATIONAL USE

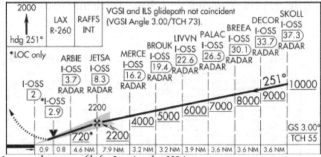

33. *Jeppesen descent profile for Los Angeles, USA*

Note the excerpt above from the approach chart. This tells the pilots the lowest possible heights to fly when at a certain distances from the airport.

For example, at a distance of 8.3 miles from the LAX 24R runway, the aircraft should be at 2,200 ft. Any lower and you risk hitting the ground, any higher and you risk having to dive down too steeply to get to the runway for a safe landing. HAL's independent GPS will detect if the aircraft is ever vertically displaced by more than a permissible distance, in which case a warning will be issued. HAL's sensitivity will be such that it will only intervene if dangerously off course.

Simulation 2 — Los Angeles

The simulation starts 9 miles from touchdown at Los Angeles on a LOC approach to runway 24R. The aircraft is being flown with the autopilot engaged, coupled with the beam that keeps the aircraft on the runway centre line but not with the vertical profile which is being controlled by the flight crew. They are at 2,200 ft on track descending in Vertical Speed mode (V/S). This mode just sets up a specific rate of descent that the pilots dial in to the autopilot but in this case the rate of descent is too high because earlier in the approach the aircraft was held high by ATC. The crew is now descending rapidly towards the airport and have estimated that they will intercept the correct glide path at 2,200 ft when at 8.3 miles from the LAX 24R runway. The visibility is 600 meters with a strong crosswind from the North while runway 24L, the very close parallel runway, is being used for takeoffs.

The aircraft does intercept the correct glide path at 2,200 ft but the crew were distracted and forgot to reduce the rate of descent to about 800 feet per minute on the autopilot panel. HAL issues the warning and the crew disconnect the autopilot and fly the aircraft level until they again intercept the correct glide path.

The approach has become "rushed" and although they are now concentrating on flying the correct vertical profile, the wind from the north has drifted the aircraft to the left and by the time they see the approach lights they are actually aligned with the parallel runway 24L that is being used for takeoffs. The crew fly a Go-Around.

34. Microsoft Flight Simulator snapshot — breaking cloud at KLAX

Although any commercial pilot may think this a bit contrived, these sorts of events do unfortunately happen as occurred on January 14, 2019 when a Saha Airlines Boeing 707 overshot the runway when landing by mistake at a close to destination but wrong airport, Fath Air Base, in Iran, killing 15. The idea is that HAL will never have to intervene...until that one time when it should.

Navigational Error Controlled Flight Into Terrain (19 fatal accidents 2010–2019)

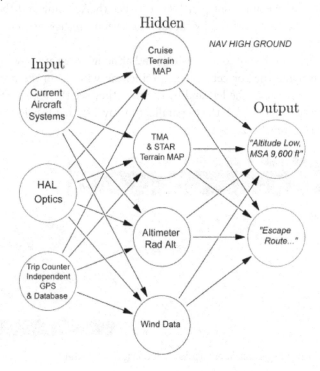

Hidden

Input

Current
Aircraft
Systems

HAL
Optics

Trip Counter
Independent
GPS
& Database

Cruise
Terrain
MAP

NAV HIGH GROUND

TMA
& STAR
Terrain MAP

Altimeter
Rad Alt

Wind Data

Output

*"Altitude Low,
MSA 9,600 ft"*

*"Escape
Route..."*

- Hidden logic — Approach Terrain Map is programmed internally and HAL tracks the descent using independent GPS and altimeter readouts. Once the aircraft descends out of the safe area, graded warnings are activated and an escape route is suggested following the published go-around routing, if possible.
- En-route Terrain Map is programmed internally together with Terminal Area (the local area surrounding the airport) terrain data and Standard Arrival chart terrain data (STAR). Wind data is monitored as increased wind strength will require greater clearance from high ground due to the possibility of increased turbulence.

Worldwide data for high ground is incorporated into the HAL database to warn against Controlled Flight Into Terrain (CFIT). Notice a mountain peak at 9,289 ft to the right of the inbound course. The airport runway elevation above sea level is 4,318 ft so obviously the aircraft will need to descend below the mountain peak to land. HAL will be programmed with allowable tolerances from this lateral inbound course to warn the pilots if they are for some reason flying below the published safety altitudes (inset showing 11,600 ft safety altitude for flying south of the KTM VOR) and on a course towards any high ground.

Chart information — Kathmandu

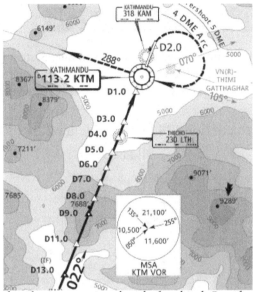

35. *Jeppesen chart showing mountain peaks and safety altitude. Reproduced with permission of Jeppesen Sanderson, Inc.*

NOT FOR NAVIGATIONAL USE

Simulation

The simulation starts approaching Kathmandu VOR/DME from the north (VOR/DME is a system that indicates the direction of the beacon relative to the aircraft and also provides distance in nautical miles). Overhead the beacon the aircraft turns left onto a heading of 150 degrees which is about south-easterly but it is flying too low for some reason at 9000 ft.

HAL has already alerted the crew that they are flying below the safety altitude.

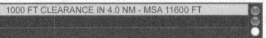

The aircraft is heading for the peak at 9,289 ft. The distance counts down and reminds the pilots of the current safety altitude.

Before the standard Ground Proximity Warning System (GPWS) activates, HAL confirms that the vertical clearance is deteriorating. This gives an important early heads up warning if the crew have become disorientated.

Runway Excursion (24 fatal accidents 2010-2019)

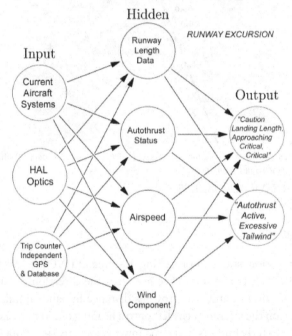

- Hidden logic — Internal runway length database referenced to check gross error on flap selection and speed using independent GPS and wind readouts. Tailwind component monitored and highlighted.
- Auto thrust monitored on PFD to warn if Auto thrust engaged but thrust not at flight idle on touchdown.

- GPS monitors runway remaining for wet conditions and reports "Caution wet," "Approaching critical wet," and/or "Critical wet." By repeatedly being informed of wet condition parameters, pilots will get a feel for the limitations of that particular runway for when eventually it is actually wet. Warnings would rarely be issued on a normal landing in dry conditions if touchdown is not too far down the runway. Slippery and reduced length runways would be more limiting and would need to be considered separately by the crew when notified in the NOTAMS (Notices to Airmen).

Simulation

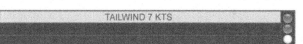

The simulation starts 4 miles from touchdown at Los Angeles on an ILS approach to runway 24R. The aircraft is being flown with the autopilot engaged, coupled to the ILS, which guides the aircraft both laterally and vertically. They are at 700 ft descending with the autothrottle engaged. This mode ensures the speed should not drop below the minimum required. The wind is variable from the north. The wind has come around resulting in a tailwind and HAL warns the crew at this time of high workload where critically it could be overlooked.

They decide to land and disconnect the Autopilot but forget to manually disengage the autothrottle. In the landing flare the power imperceptibly increases as the autothrust system is now trying to keep the speed at the minimum approach speed. The aircraft doesn't touch down, using up valuable runway distance.

HAL reminds the crew that if the runway were wet, the critical touchdown point is close and they could be risking a runway excursion.

The alert is upgraded to a warning as they near the critical point.

APPROACHING WET CRITICAL LANDING LENGTH

The crew disengage the autothrottle and place the aircraft firmly on the runway to ensure the braking system has maximum effect. They taxi off at the very end of the runway.

Engine Failure (19 fatal accidents 2010–2019)

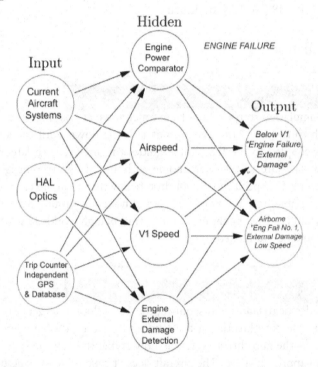

- Hidden logic — Power comparator detects engine failure below V1 (Stop/Go decision speed) on takeoff. If fire or damage is detected externally, warnings are issued to assist decision making regarding possible passenger evacuation.
- After V1, if fire or damage is detected externally, a warning is issued to assist decision making regarding immediate return. External camera/detector permanently monitors the video stream looking for irregularities in the engine and the wing area.
- Airspeed permanently monitored to ensure speed does not decay below V2 (Engine out minimum speed) which could cause control loss.

Simulation

The simulation starts 5 miles after takeoff from Montreal Trudeau International airport 06L, Canada. The aircraft is being flown manually and the left engine is about to fail in an uncontained manner which causes subsequent damage to the wing leading edges.

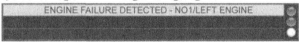

HAL Power comparator identifies the failed engine having crosschecked with other parameters.

External detector warns of damage.

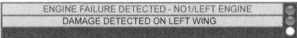

Detector finds irregularity in video stream and deduces that the leading edge could have been damaged. Also warns of any speed decay, taking into consideration the rate of speed decrease due to the power loss on one engine.

Microburst/Windshear/Instrument failures (13 fatal accidents 2010–2019)

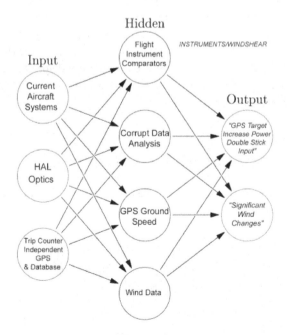

- Hidden logic — GPS speed and wind data warns of significant wind changes to act as a preliminary warning before the current onboard Windshear system is activated. The alert would be useful in any phase of flight to ensure the aircraft is kept on the optimum flight path and particularly during the approach phase to ensure a stable approach.

- Monitoring of the 3 Attitude indicators confirms to the pilots which one has failed and which one should be followed. Similar monitoring would occur for the Altimeters, Heading indicator and Airspeed indicators.

- Multiple failures logic provides essential instructions to stay within the flight envelope.

Simulation

The simulation starts at 37,000 ft over Montreal, Canada when all airspeed indications are lost. This is shortly followed by failures in altitude readout.

HAL detects that all airspeed information has been lost or is corrupt and prioritizes the multiple warnings appearing on the ECAM/EICAS display to provide essential information only. Current GPS altitude and target GPS groundspeed is immediately provided together with wind information. The target speed is 554 kts over the ground taking into account the aircraft is experiencing a 47 kts tailwind, but the actual ground speed is only 534 kts meaning they need to increase speed or risk a stall. At high altitudes these small speed margins can be critical.

Real time updates assist the crew to maintain situational awareness. If wind data is not available, HAL uses last known wind data or will download and interpret the best available data.

Power indicators give essential guidance.

Sensors on sidesticks alert the crew to control input conflicts.

38300 FT - G/S TARGET 554 KTS (47 KT TAIL) - G/S NOW 510 KTS
GPS ALTITUDE NOW 38300 FT
DOUBLE SIDESTICK INPUT

Go-Around/Somatogravic Illusion (10 fatal accidents 2010–2019)

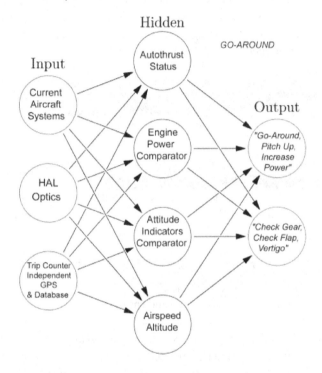

- Hidden logic — Auto thrust status and power settings are monitored to ensure Go-around power is set. Power comparator reminds pilots if an engine has failed to prevent against control loss.
- Altitude, Airspeed and Attitude indicators monitored to ensure Go-around maneuver is not delayed and is positively executed.
- Attitude indicators monitored to ensure pilot has not succumbed to somatogravic illusion (Vertigo is caused by acceleration of the aircraft whilst turning the head). Alert and claxon issued if excessive pitch down detected.

Simulation

The simulation starts 4 miles from touchdown at Los Angeles on an ILS approach to runway 24R on a dark overcast night. The aircraft is being flown with the autopilot engaged, coupled to the ILS, which guides the aircraft both laterally and vertically. The aircraft breaks cloud and the landing pilot disconnects the autopilot and the autothrottle as the approach lights come into view to manually land the aircraft. It immediately becomes clear that there is another aircraft on the runway and so they initiate the manual Go-Around procedure but going straight back into cloud and darkness, the handling pilot pitches up very slowly.

HAL detects slow pitch rate and issues an alert.

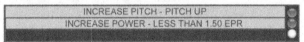

Not used to executing manual Go-arounds without the autothrottle, the power setting is incorrect. The distraction makes them forget about the Gear and Flap.

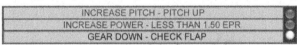

HAL issues a reminder of the flap and the gear.

The gear has still been overlooked but the pilot flying the go-around now looks to the left at his letdown plate to check the correct course for the overshoot procedure. When he looks forward again, he is affected by somatogravic illusion or vertigo and perceives that the aircraft is violently pitching up. The nose is lowered at an excessive rate.

HAL senses the high rate of pitch reduction and, with the trip counter knowing the aircraft is in a Go-around, issues an alert together with an attention-getting claxon.

Flight Deck Lock Out/Suicide (5 fatal accidents 2010-2019)

• Hidden logic — Personnel detector senses only 1 person in the locked flight deck. HAL automatically unlocks the flight deck door for any situation that requires the assistance of the other pilot, for example; abnormally large altitude change commanded through the autopilot system or autopilot disconnected and large rate of descent detected or the aircraft descends, even at a low rate, through 20,000 ft above the area safety altitude.

• The same logic applies if any unusual selections are made on the flight deck including an engine or further engines being shutdown, fuel jettison, pressurization controls selected, cameras blocked or specific readouts on the PFD/ND/EICAS are covered over. A discrete chime sounds in the passenger cabin to alert the entire crew.

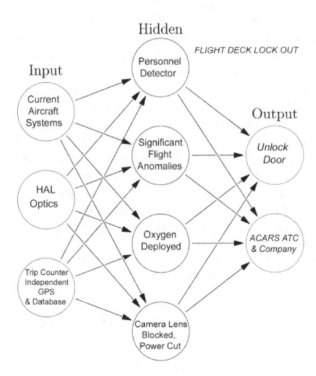

Simulation

The simulation starts at 25,000 ft above Montreal, Canada. One of the pilots leaves the flight deck. A check is made on the currently installed post 9/11 security camera, monitoring the galley area to ensure no passengers are close to the flight deck door; the pilot opens the door which locks behind him. In fact the aircraft has no passengers aboard and is on a test flight to check out the new security system. The aircraft will make several maneuvers to check HAL will release the door when any unusual flight patterns or flight deck selections are detected.

DOOR LOCKED — The current safety altitude below is 3,300 ft and the aircraft will shortly descend from 25,000 ft for a lower altitude. Estimated Top of Descent point for destination is many miles away.

DOOR OPEN — Passing through 23,300 ft, only 1 person is detected on the flight deck so the door is released by HAL as certain important conditions have been met. The door would remain locked after the normal Top of Descent point but if descended early, the door will open. If there were a pilot incapacitation, then a cabin crew member would come to the flight deck to assist the incapacitated pilot as well as to help with any requests from the other pilot, like reading the checklist. If in an emergency situation a pilot needed to observe a problem from the cabin, like to check if the flaps have fully extended, then a cabin crew member would be called to the flight deck so HAL would detect 2 people and thus keep the door firmly locked. If the sole pilot at the controls then sets up an irregular flight path, the cabin crew member would simply physically open the door for the other pilot. HAL also removes the vulnerability of cabin crew who a terrorist may incorrectly assume have special access codes or keys to the flight deck door.

DOOR LOCKED — The aircraft is back at 25,000 ft and now the aircraft is accelerated towards maximum speed.

DOOR OPEN — Only one person is detected on the flight deck. As excessive speed is very undesirable, HAL opens the door together with the discrete chime in the cabin to alert the crew.

DOOR LOCKED — The aircraft is back at 25,000 ft and now the gear is selected down — DOOR OPEN

DOOR LOCKED — The aircraft is back at 25,000 ft and now the flaps are selected down — DOOR OPEN

DOOR LOCKED — Now an engine is shutdown — DOOR OPEN

DOOR LOCKED — The cabin is depressurized — DOOR OPEN

DOOR LOCKED — Fuel starts jettisoning out of the wing tips — DOOR OPEN

DOOR LOCKED — The HAL camera is covered over — DOOR OPEN

DOOR LOCKED — The Speed indications on the PFD are blocked with the checklist — DOOR OPEN

There is another purposely withheld sequence that is required in unison with this system to safeguard against other sinister combinations. The list goes on, transforming the flight deck door into a quasi-intelligent two way system.

Total Engine Power Loss (4 fatal accidents 2010–2019)

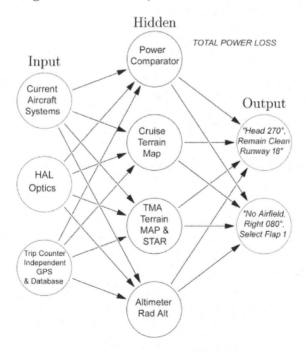

Hidden logic
- Power comparator detects total power loss.
- Independent GPS, altitude data and internal Route Terrain Map calculates closest airfield and/or steers aircraft away from high ground.
- Approach chart and Terrain data are utilized by HAL to provide headings for the most suitable landing site.
- Altitude and Wind data provide cues for speed reduction and flap selection taking into consideration increased time required for exten-sion due to reduced hydraulic pressure available after total power loss.

Simulation

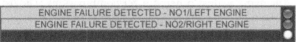

ENGINE FAILURE DETECTED - NO1/LEFT ENGINE
ENGINE FAILURE DETECTED - NO2/RIGHT ENGINE

The simulation starts at 25,000 ft above Montreal, Trudeau International airport, Canada. The aircraft is approaching a large flock of migrating birds.

Once HAL detects a total power loss it concentrates on the location of the forced landing. HAL picks another airfield in Montreal other than the closer but busier Trudeau International.

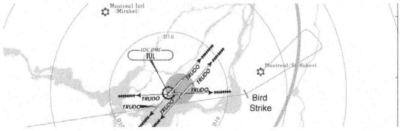

36. Jeppesen chart showing point of bird strike and HAL routing into Montreal St Hubert. Reproduced with permission of Jeppesen Sanderson, Inc.

NOT FOR NAVIGATIONAL USE

The crew declares a "Mayday" giving their intentions to land at St Hubert (CYHU) and ATC coordinate allowing the crew time to attempt engine re-lights whilst following the optimum flight path for landing. The distance to run information is live and counting down.

CYHU 24R OPTIMUM - LOADING DESCENT WINDS
HEADING 070 - SPEED MIN CLEAN
FLAP 1 IN 14 MILES

HAL shares the mental picture with the crew.

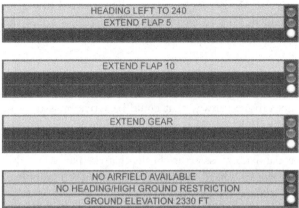

When no suitable airfield is available, relevant information is displayed and HAL avoids high ground where possible whilst heading for flat terrain.

Incorrect Takeoff Flap (1 fatal accident 2010–2019)

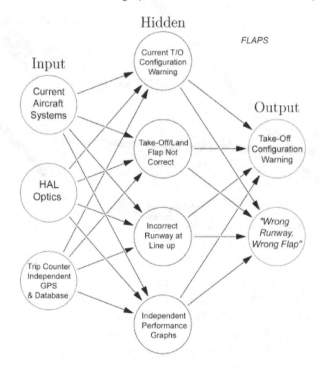

• Hidden logic — HAL detects the takeoff flap selected in unison with the independent GPS to ensure the correct flap is set as the aircraft approaches the takeoff point proximate to the runway.

• GPS will ensure the aircraft is lined up with the correct runway for takeoff to prevent low visibility taxiing errors. It will also ensure the aircraft does not cross a runway that could be active by issuing an appropriate warning.

• Independent database gross error checks that the flap selected is sufficient for the runway ahead and when ¾ takeoff power is applied, will alert the crew if not.

• Same logic is used for Landing flaps and landing runway identification.

Chart Information — Montreal

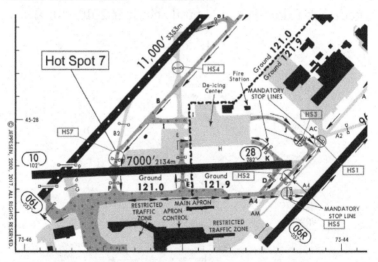

37. *Jeppesen chart showing Hot Spots at Montreal International where taxiing incidents are likely to occur. NOT FOR NAVIGATIONAL USE*

This is the airfield plate for Montreal, Trudeau International airport, Canada and is a diagram of the airfield used by pilots to enable them to safely follow taxi instructions from Air Traffic Control, especially in low visibility. The runways are shown in black and the taxiways in grey. Runway incursion hot spots are marked by small circles named HS1 to HS8 and represent the critical danger areas during operations in fog and low visibility conditions.

Simulation

The simulation starts on taxiway Bravo ("B") approaching runway 10/28 at what is published on the chart as Hot Spot 7. The intention is to cross runway 10/28 at Bravo, clearing the other side on Foxtrot and then to turn right towards Golf where the aircraft will line up on 06L for takeoff. The visibility is 600 meters and runway 06L is one of the active departure runways but there is a small jet ahead taxiing for a departure off runway 10.

APPROACHING RUNWAY 10/28 - 150M

Alert displayed approaching Hot Spot 7 as a small jet departs runway 10.

GROUNDSPEED > 25 KTS

Having turned right onto a downward slope, parallel to runway 10/28, HAL warns of excessive taxiing ground speed.

APPROACHING RUNWAY 06L - 150M

Alert displayed approaching runway 06L.

Turning onto 06L a radio transmission distracts the crew and the aircraft lines up with runway 10 by mistake. The HAL GPS confirms the error but does not activate as in this case the threshold lat/long is shared for both runway 10 and 06L and would have raised a "nuisance" warning if no line up error had occurred or the aircraft was stopped close to the runway awaiting a preceding aircraft to depart. But when ¾ power is applied for takeoff . . .

38. Microsoft Flight Simulator snapshot — lining up for runway 06 or 10 at Montreal International. Reproduced with permission of Jeppesen Sanderson, Inc. NOT FOR NAVI-GATIONAL USE

... the crew are alerted to the mistake as the heading is inconsistent with the planned takeoff runway QDM or magnetic track direction of the runway as per the ND display.

The takeoff is rejected and the aircraft clears runway 10 at Foxtrot where the crew carry out the after landing checklist, raising the flap. They approach runway 06L for a second time.

This time the aircraft lines up with the correct runway (06L) and an alert is issued for the flaps which have not been selected down, as the crew are now out of their normal sequence and have forgotten to re-run the takeoff checklist.

Correct takeoff flap is set and the takeoff checklist is completed, reverting the HAL interface to what will mostly be observed in normal operations.

Other HAL Interventions and Detectors

39. 747-400 wing on landing showing reverse thrust, leading edge flaps and lift dump

Many other systems would be monitored by HAL, for example fuel state to guard against possible fuel leaks. Speed limitations for flaps, gear and many more useful interventions can be programmed into the system and eventually HAL could be further expanded to allow monitoring for external dangers around the aircraft. We have already mentioned damage detection on the wing around the engines.

This is an important area where an uncontained engine failure involving failed high speed turbine blades could cause serious problems. Ice can form on wings, engines can catch fire, cowlings can become displaced, flaps and leading edge devices can become damaged or stuck and ground personnel can be sucked into engines on the tarmac even at relatively low power settings.

External Detectors

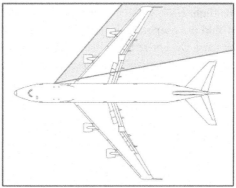

40. Camera/detector coverage of 747-400 wing

The external monitors would be multipurpose to detect ice, fire, people and damage. It would need to detect heat and moving objects but would also need to compare the normal, expected picture, to one where an engine has lost a cowling or where damage has been inflicted to a leading edge. A perfect "single job" use for AI that has been so successful in the detection of lung cancer cells. The word "Damage" would be annunciated and when the crew have time they would observe from the passenger cabin. The ice detection system would be primarily for turboprop aircraft that can suffer badly. It would need a sophisticated detector to reliably sense even small build-ups of ice. They would be designed to be so sensitive that they would warn before the aircraft attempts to takeoff and when airborne it would warn of icing to alert the pilots to engage the anti-ice systems as soon as possible. Serious ice buildup, although rare, has caused aircraft to literally fall out of the sky.

A single housing, multipurpose detector could be fitted to any aircraft to at least warn the crew of an impending problem. Even on a large jet, extended taxiing at a busy international airport can put the aircraft at risk from icing so a critically calibrated system would benefit all aviation across the board.

If physical damage is detected externally, the warning could critically assist decision making regarding immediate return. If leading or trailing edge flaps were damaged, the warning could prevent the crew from doing what is correct in normal practice, but could subsequently be fatal. If the aircraft reduced speed after an engine failure on takeoff to climb away at the optimum rate, it could stall the wing if the leading edge or trailing edge flaps had been damaged by the uncontained explosion. The same detector would monitor for ground personnel if they were standing too close to the engines during start or ground runs.

All of this would only enhance HAL but would not be necessary for its primary function within the flight deck, although the Personnel detector would have to be an integral part of the system. It needs to sense how many persons are on the flight deck with the door locked at any one time. As we have seen, this would be a separate camera/detector positioned to be able to observe and/or sense the entire flight deck area and would probably use video, infrared, motion detection and image recognition analysis.

Sidestick Detectors

Detection is required for sidestick manipulation on either side. Probably the best solution would be a pressure switch on the sidestick so that the system will know when both sidesticks are being operated at the same time. This would not interfere with normal Airbus protocols; HAL isn't meant to interpose with current systems and will only raise an issue if other more limiting factors come into play.

Trapping Errors

This whole chapter has dealt with the last 10 years (2010–2019) of accidents and it may seem an excessive amount of work introducing a new system to combat these rare eventualities. Every accident must be seen as avoidable and HAL will need to consider a complete history of aviation accidents and incidents (see appendix) to ensure it has solutions pre-loaded. It will also need to look ahead to try and predict the next set of awkward combinations that are almost certain to occur, especially with the introduction of new aircraft designs.

Error on Error

This will be a very important part of the overall logic. If a speed readout on the pilot's PFD is incorrect due to an iced up pitot tube then this reading needs to be rejected. As in the human brain, we need to look at several related inputs and then decide on which one to believe. Onboard there are 3 airspeed indicator systems that each independently calculate the airspeed of the aircraft through the air. Unfortunately, if there is severe icing outside then all three sensors can become useless.

A GPS system will regardless be able to indicate the speed of the aircraft but if the aircraft is flying into a 100 kts headwind then there will be a disparity. However these days there are many hundreds of aircraft flying the world's airways and they continually provide the Meteorological office with the crucial wind information at various altitudes. Until the wind data is received, HAL will use the last recorded wind from the IRS (Inertial Reference System) that normally provides accurate navigational information to the aircraft. Upper wind information is crucial to airlines as they don't like burning unnecessary fuel en route and knowing the exact winds aloft allows them to calculate the fuel required very accurately. This is a good thing for the planet and explains why your flight to the UK from the USA is always so bumpy — the aircraft is routed down the nearest jet stream blowing at up to 200 mph.

So now we can download the winds from satellites and provide reasonable enough data to prevent an aircraft from losing control. As HAL is an independently powered system, it won't be contaminated by any confused data coming from the onboard computers. Just as the human brain can detect anomalies on the flight deck, HAL will be programmed to look for specific disagreements on the pilot flight displays to prioritize essential information for the crew.

If specific parameter readouts are blocked on the PFD, HAL can differentiate between a blockage and missing or corrupted data due to a fault or failure. So if the captain's speed readout is in disagreement with the first officer's side then HAL can work out which one is in error by looking at the many other parameters available. If the readout goes blank then the null recorded by HAL is registered as a disconnect as opposed to a block.

CHAPTER 8: EVOLUTION BEFORE FULL AUTOMATION

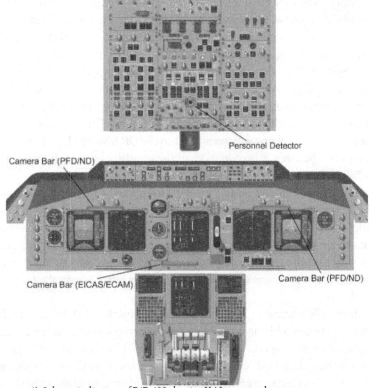

41. Schematic diagram of 747-400 showing HAL camera placements

Do we need to evolve a little further and develop a better computer/ human symbiosis before we embrace full automation? The HAL flight test Application works well but there is one obvious drawback — the camera needs to be positioned so it can read all the computer LCD screens at the same time. In this chapter I will look at how this may be achieved.

Two camera bars, one either side, would read data from the PFD and ND. Another camera bar would read data from the EICAS/ECAM from below. The camera system obviously cannot block the view of the pilot but if placed strategically around the edges of the computer LCD screen, HAL could use correction algorithms to decode the distortion as if it were aligned directly in front. All the cameras can be linked/networked together and the HAL inter-face, providing information to each pilot, could be positioned on top of the camera bar housing.

However problems still exist with regard to sunlight glare and line of sight being blocked at the critical moment. There also needs to be a slight delay built into the software to ensure the program has correctly interpreted the words or digits... much like pilots undergo at their bi-annual medical check.

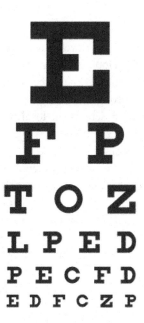

As we go down the eyesight chart we need more time to analyze the shapes. Is it a Q or an O, a D or a Q? Guessing won't help and if we do use a suspect result in a critical decision, we may cause more problems than we solve. We do, though, have the advantage that a weather forecaster has at their disposal in as much as an accurate forecast is much easier to predict given that the overall weather synopsis has already been observed for the previous day. So, as in my health App mentioned earlier, if the speech synthesis returned "you'll get," I could exchange the words for "yoghurt" which the App would recognize because I know we are only looking for foodstuffs.

With HAL, we know what we are expecting to be critical so if the system mistakenly read CABIN ATTITUDE, we can override and replace the word with the correct version, CABIN ALTITUDE. This mimics the human brain where we may doubt the first thing we heard or read and so will start processing the likely possibilities before we accept the most plausible fit.

The HAL App does cope pretty well with varying light settings and reflection off the simulator monitor but improvements need to be made for it to work in the real world. Most importantly the HAL App proves that Heavy pilot emulation can work, providing another pair of virtual eyes in the flight deck to enhance safety throughout the entire flight.

Solutions

The solution I propose for development is a photo-sensitive plastic overlay screen which would look similar to a smart phone screen protector. We are all familiar with these screen protectors which conveniently allow a touch to be transmitted through the special plastic so the smart phone can react. The touch screen then detects the local coordinates of the touch and the software responds. So if the touch was over a virtual button, then that particular procedure or routine is activated.

The photo-sensitive plastic overlay screen would act as a touch-sensitive screen in reverse. Instead of a touch being recognized as a voltage in a particular area of the screen on the smart phone, this new plastic overlay would recognize the LCD light output from the smart phone screen and relay the result to the HAL computer.

Any word or character output to the LCD would interact with the plastic screen and be fed out through connections to the HAL processor. This way we don't have to consider camera alignment, blockages, lighting conditions or malicious interference.

So, the pilot will interpret the usual data from the PFD, coming through the plastic overlay but at the same time HAL will also interpret the very same data (plus more) and assist where necessary.

43. Flexible computer screen technology

Earlier in the book I alluded to two other important advantages of the HAL system. Although the aviation world is dominated by Boeing and Airbus there are several other types flying around — ATR, Embraer, Sukhoi, Bombardier, de Havilland Canada, Beechcraft, CASA, Cessna, Fairchild Swearingen to name a few and could all be integrated with HAL without undue complication. The two advantages are:

- HAL can be integrated with any existing aircraft type with flat screen displays.
- The installation is totally independent from the existing technology of the "tried and tested" aircraft type.

This second point is important because any additions, how ever minor, that are bolted on to the original design can have unexpected and undesirable consequences causing failures where there were none before. There has to be time-consuming, extensive testing before any amendments are certified by the authorities otherwise metaphorically, these additions can lead to a collapse of our House of Cards.

If the onboard computer systems are left to operate as they were designed and we now add an independent layer, we have the desired balanced result we were seeking — no one part being stacked dangerously high with too much riding on it.

Human *Computer* *HAL (Human/Computer)*

From here on, we'll call the photo-sensitive plastic overlay screen a "Photo-Sensitive Screen" or PSS. It will be comprised of a thin, transparent flexible plastic sheet that is cut to fit exactly over the pilot displays. So, one for the PFD, one for the ND and one each for the upper and lower EICAS/ECAM. On the edges of the PSS will be flat cable wires that take the signals to the central HAL processor. The pilots fly the aircraft through the usual displays, visible through the PSS, and at the same time HAL interprets the very same display just as a Heavy pilot would do to enhance the safety of the flight.

It will work like a regular computer screen but in reverse. Instead of the characters being sent out to the screen and the words, numbers and graphics displayed on the monitor, the PSS detects the exact shape of the lit LCD pixels below and sends the pixel shape through the flat cable to the HAL processor to be decoded to characters.

44. Flexible computer screen showing output connections

Critically, this isolates HAL from the aircraft flight displays, preventing any negative backward interference into the aircraft systems or forward contamination of corrupt data into the HAL computer. Separate specific software then integrates pilot and computer perceptions — the HAL computer. The idea is to recreate the human synapse we discussed in an earlier chapter which has evolved to control the impulses from the brain to the toe. If the speed indications on the PFD suddenly increase, instead of a hard wired knee-jerk reaction of slamming the thrust levers closed, it allows for a more intelligent analysis.

Air France 447 could very well have had a different outcome with HAL looking for clues that pointed towards a pitot tube icing failure. By sensing the associated multiple failures, a completely different, independent set of programming rules would have come into play to initially provide the crew with only the most essential information. Asiana Airlines Flight 214, descending into San Francisco would have HAL permanently monitoring the autothrottle annunciations on the flight displays and together with a real time analysis of the speed readout would have alerted the crew.

1.0	1.0	1.0	0.8	0.6	0.6	0.6	0.8	1.0	1.0	1.0	1.0
1.0	0.5	0.0	0.0	0.0	0.0	0.0	0.0	0.5	1.0	1.0	1.0
1.0	0.0	0.0	0.5	0.6	0.6	0.5	0.0	0.0	0.5	1.0	1.0
1.0	1.0	1.0	1.0	1.0	1.0	1.0	1.0	0.0	0.0	1.0	1.0
1.0	1.0	1.0	1.0	1.0	1.0	1.0	1.0	0.5	0.0	0.8	1.0
1.0	1.0	1.0	0.5	0.5	0.5	0.5	0.5	0.4	0.0	0.5	1.0
1.0	0.5	0.0	0.0	0.0	0.0	0.0	0.0	0.0	0.0	0.5	1.0
0.8	0.0	0.0	0.5	1.0	1.0	1.0	1.0	0.0	0.5	0.0	0.5	1.0
0.5	0.0	0.5	1.0	1.0	1.0	1.0	1.0	0.0	0.5	0.0	0.5	1.0
0.5	0.0	0.6	1.0	1.0	1.0	1.0	1.0	0.0	0.0	0.0	0.5	1.0
0.5	0.0	0.5	1.0	1.0	1.0	1.0	1.0	0.0	0.5	0.0	0.5	1.0
0.8	0.0	0.0	0.5	0.6	0.6	0.5	0.0	0.4	0.0	0.5	1.0
1.0	0.8	0.0	0.0	0.0	0.0	0.0	0.8	0.5	0.0	0.5	1.0
1.0	1.0	1.0	0.6	0.6	0.6	1.0	1.0	1.0	1.0	1.0	1.0

45. The letter "a" as displayed on a computer screen with pixel decode on the right.

Any computer screen is comprised of hundreds of pixels with each character having a different layout and therefore a different set of codes. The image above shows the makeup of the lowercase letter "a":

We just need to reverse engineer the process of pressing the letter "a" on the keyboard. The PSS system will effectively read the intensity of each pixel and provide a grid of codes as seen on the right side of the above diagram. This will then be fed to the processor to identify the letter "a."

It may appear a bit strange going through all this effort to just read off the text that is clearly available as a computer code at the time it is sent to the PFD screen. In the case of the letter "a," the standard computer code is 97 and you might ask why we can't just tap into the aircraft computer just before its processor sends out the code 97 to the graphics card. There are 2 major reasons as to why this would not be desirable:

- The first problem is that we are now relying on the computer outputs to provide data for flight information to the pilots as well as vital crosscheck data for HAL. If the ships computers fail, as has happened with pitot tube icing, then HAL gets mixed in with the faulty data running around the system and becomes equally confused. By keeping HAL separate it can crosscheck other parameters to see what has shutdown or what is now providing unintelligible data to come to a quasi human like conclusion of what has occurred. Another way of looking at it might be when we consider computer viruses. As we know, once a virus gets into a computer it can irretrievably shut it down, normally until the user pays a random. The PSS/HAL setup allows it to act like a firewall — there is no way to get into the HAL processor from the ships computer and vice-versa.
- The extra connections required to link in HAL directly to the ship's computers only adds to the overall level of complication of the system and would be the equivalent of building another few layers of cards on our computer House of Cards. This means that we are now raising the odds that we will have a failure within the system by over-complicating the very same system!

As we mentioned before, this isolation of the two computer systems is a mirroring of the human synapse we spoke of in the earlier chapter on Evolutionary Aspects. Synapses only allow electrical flow in one direction. Without synapses, the central nervous system would be under constant bombardment with impulses which would cause central nervous system fatigue. The responses would be slow and reverse flow of impulses would lead to uncoordinated functioning — or the dreaded blue screen of death! By isolating one computer from the other, we mimic the human synapse by stopping backward data flow, which could crash the system. By allowing the summation of all relevant inputs from various displays, we generate a meaningful, weighted response.

In practical terms, PSS will stop the primary onboard computers from contaminating the HAL software, allowing the system to offer essential guidance to the pilots in a catastrophic situation. For instance, if any flight display speed indication fails, the *Integration System* (HAL) can use other

readouts (neuron routings) to ascertain that the pilot needs other meaningful information regarding speed. This will effectively result in an alternative array of synapses opening to present GPS ground speed information,
integrated with wind data.

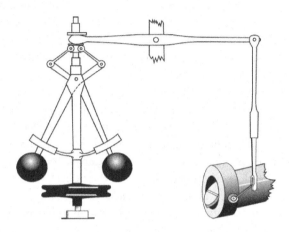

46. Steam Engine Flyball Governor

Its overall effect will be similar to the function of a steam Governor that
balanced the system in a Victorian steam engine. When the engine runs
too fast, the rotating weighted balls fly out under centrifugal force which
compresses the apparatus on the left, pulling down the central cross linkage.
This in turn moves a valve which reduces the steam pressure so the machine
then runs a little slower. Equally, when the pressure is raised on the flight
deck due to serious failures, HAL is activated to offer essential information
to the crew, enabling them to recover and return the situation to normal.

So how might this computer synapse system work practically? Imagine
we are flying along quite happily at 35,000 ft in a 747-400. The weather is
perfect and there is no turbulence. Suddenly we lose all airspeed information
— it just goes blank on the captain's instruments, the first officer's instruments and the standby instruments. The regular onboard computer systems
will now issue several warnings to get the attention of the pilots so they
can deal with the problem. But what the current system is really saying is
that the computer program has been contaminated with unknown data. It
may be receiving a continuous sequence of zeros, a value of 10.9 or a quick
flash of 1, 3004,023 followed by the letter "a" and depending on the fault, the
airspeed may return and then disappear again. The programmers know that
these errors need to be trapped to avoid a total system crash so they write

in several lines of code to ensure the processor(s) doesn't hang up as could happen if an illegal computation was executed during the fault condition.

If we link HAL directly to the airspeed outputs, HAL will just become a part of the confusion, trying to work out if the airspeed inputs are genuine. What we want HAL to do is register that the captain's airspeed is out of limits, crosscheck it with the first officer's airspeed indication, note the power setting, note the fuel state (to calculate the aircraft weight), note the altitude, note the flap setting, note the pitch attitude of the aircraft, note the undercarriage selection and much more.

Now HAL will look up the "Flight with unreliable airspeed" table which normally sits within one of the onboard aircraft flight manuals. Here we crosscheck altitude with aircraft weight and read off the correct engine power setting and required flight pitch angle to maintain level flight within the correct tolerances of airspeed. In the case above, HAL will note that no parameters are close to critical, thanks to the perfect weather conditions, advise that all airspeed input has been lost, confirm target power settings and attitude for level flight and backup with an independent GPS speed readout with last known wind component.

Suppose, though, that it was only the captain's airspeed readout which was playing up. We expect a sensible, "weighted" response so HAL will crosscheck the first officer's airspeed, note it is highly likely to be correct by comparison to the "Flight with unreliable airspeed" table and independent GPS, to issue guidance as to which airspeed indicator to ignore — remember, the captain's airspeed readout might be only 20 kts out but nevertheless dangerously inaccurate for flight at 35, 000 ft. For completeness, current systems are designed to raise an alert for airspeed disparity between the two sides but it's up to the pilots to decide which one is correct.

The PSS (Photo-Sensitive Screen), as well as being transparent, would need to be flexible and be able to fit a variety of different screen sizes found in glass cockpits. The HAL computer would encompass the independent GPS and connections to the Personnel camera/detector and the flight deck door locking mechanism. It won't need to be any larger than a typical smart phone and could be easily hidden behind a panel where it would be protected from possible sabotage. Another connection would link HAL to the external detector unit, as previously mentioned, to further protect the aircraft.

Color detection will assist in ascertaining the urgency of a situation following the normal protocols of the aircraft systems thus providing more "weighting" to the HAL neural network. For instance, the words CABIN ALTITUDE (warning of a cabin depressurization) will not be instantly reacted upon by HAL until the weightings increase to trigger an action potential with additions of color detection and cabin altitude, cabin rate and bleed air duct pressure readings on the EICAS/ECAM display. HAL will use all these data inputs together with an array of other related readings before reacting.

The PSS will read numbers and characters in specific areas of the flight deck display and by knowing the grid reference of where this information is displayed, the HAL computer will be able to decipher its context. This ability can be expanded to include the tracking of shapes on a display. Pilots use the Artificial Horizon on their Primary Flight Display (PFD) to know whether the aircraft is pitching or turning. HAL will detect if any pitch or turn is excessive and also whether the rate of pitch or turn is worthy of a mention by the non-handling pilot. As HAL is designed as "Heavy Aircrew Logic," it will regardlessly annunciate a suitable warning.

The Artificial Horizon and other types of data displayed to the pilots are essential when flying in cloud so sensing these readouts is a vital tool for monitoring. However, one other type of sensing can be equally important — the ability to sense nothing. Missing data can give a big clue as to which aircraft systems may have failed and HAL will detect any absence of data that the pilots normally expect to be present.

The HAL trip counter will use all the same cues from the PFDs, NDs and EICAS/ECAM to determine which phase of flight the aircraft is currently experiencing. By monitoring the late stages of an approach and tracking the radio altimeter, barometric altimeter, rate of descent and speed, the trip counter will sense whether to transition from approach phase into landing phase or transfer into the more critical Go-around phase.

Power for HAL would be supplied via the aircraft battery which is always available even if all the engines have failed and therefore cannot run the ships electrical generators. The system could then be even more independent if it were further isolated by inductive charging so it would remain active even if the aircraft battery is disconnected in an incident or a fire.

Other functionality that we are used to these days is the ability to update our smart phones with data and software. As HAL is independent from the aircraft systems, it will be able to download software updates en route as well as the latest information about the destination or alternate. I've never downloaded an update to my smart phone that goes on to completely crash the system, as the companies that write the operating systems know very well that great care needs to be taken to avoid a critical error. With the same amount of care, and bearing in mind that HAL is not the first line of defense but a backup to the aircraft systems, we can introduce other helpful dimensions to HAL. For instance, if an alternate airfield is closed due to bad weather, HAL will be able to communicate this to the pilots in a timely manner via the HAL interface.

Below is the entire schematic for the HAL installation on the Boeing 747-400. The small HAL computer would be tucked away behind the instrument panels and the complete installation would be practically indistinguishable from the fight deck we have today.

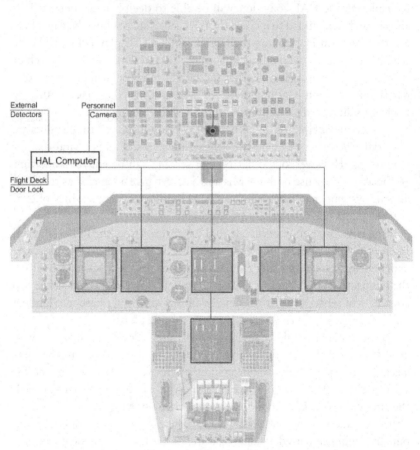

47. Schematic diagram of 747-400 showing HAL connections

Chapter 9: Extended Applications

This second layer of the HAL weighted analysis would mainly be applicable for industries that have similar vulnerabilities to aviation that, in extremis, risk life and limb. However, money has always proved to be quite high on the preservation list and there may be a case for the virus protection quality of HAL to assist in limiting hacking attacks of sensitive computer systems in our security and banking sectors. This chapter deals with a few examples that could benefit, starting with hospital monitors for which I have also written a demonstration Android App.

Medical

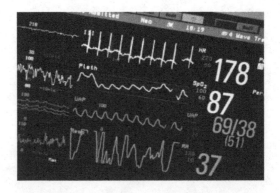

48. Vital Signs of Heart rate, Blood pressure, Oxygen saturation and Respiration rate

Alarm fatigue is sensory overload when clinicians are exposed to an excessive number of alarms, which can result in desensitisation to alarms and missed alarms. Patient deaths have been attributed to this phenomenon.[2]

The quote above is from an on-line article concerning alarm fatigue issues in hospitals. Even if a hospital has all the latest equipment and all of their patients are connected to monitors, there's still that catch 22 to overcome. With a photo-sensitive plastic overlay screen (PSS) connected to HAL, patients would be monitored 24/7 but now with an ability to analyze the outputs for known issues. It sends a text notification to a clinician if anything untoward is detected.

The App simulation involves a PC emulating a hospital monitor which is programmed to randomly alter the vital signs of heart rate, blood pressure, oxygen saturation, respiration rate and temperature. The smart phone (HAL) will be interpreting the outputs and sending a 'patient specific' text message if and when the vital signs reach preset limits. HAL also detects if the monitoring attachments on the patient have failed or have become detached.

Notification 12:33 — Stats Check Bed 9

Notification 03:17 — Blood Pressure Sensor Error Ward B, Bed 2

49. Medical staff receive instant alerts

[2] https://pubmed.ncbi.nlm.nih.gov/24153215/

In a large hospital it may be better to utilize a centralized unit where one person would monitor all notifications and then contact the relevant clinician. This way, if a nurse or doctor was dealing with another emergency, the alert notification would not be overlooked.

Independent programming within HAL would set graded limits to warn of a patient's specific vulnerabilities. E.g. a 10% high/low warning.

Notification 13:17 — Blood Pressure 10% Inc 160/90, Bed 7

Notification 23:17 — Oxygen Saturation Low 94%, Bed 4

Notification 06:17 — Heart rate Low 50 bpm, Bed 2

50. Personnel detector guards against missing patients

The personnel detector, similar to the one we introduced for the aviation application, would be attached to the side of the monitor looking towards the patient to guard against the not so rare problem of patients going missing! A time delay would be set to allow for regular bathroom visits.

Notification 18:24 — Missing Patient Bed 5

Hospitals worldwide wouldn't necessarily need to replace existing monitors so regularly in order to stay up to date with newly introduced functionality like analysis and communication. Provided the current equipment is working, HAL/PSS can be integrated, as shown below, to deliver the updated functionality of a new state-of-the-art monitor. This should cut down the cost of buying in the latest model of monitor which could be very expensive for large hospitals, and would certainly be a good option for less affluent parts of the world that cannot afford to regularly upgrade.

The PSS is fitted over the monitor screen to read the vital sign outputs from the patient. The data is connected to the HAL computer on the rear of the monitor via flat cable wires and a small webcam/detector is attached to the flat cable, facing forward to check if the patient is still present. Bluetooth, Wi-Fi, USB and Text connectivity allow for easy update and transmission of notifications. Password protection ensures HAL remains synchronized with the specific monitor and patient.

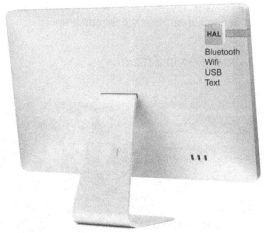

51. *The HAL computer fitted to an existing monitor*

Power would be supplied via the monitor mains supply but would be isolated by inductive charging so the HAL computer will remain active even if there is a mains power failure — clinicians will be alerted to such failures by HAL's ability to sense absence of readout or data on the monitor.

Railways

52. *Similar aviation safeguards in the drivers cab*

The functionality for the railways, both signaling and powered rolling stock, would be very similar to the application in aviation. In 2013, a train derailed on a bend at "Santiago de Compostela" in Spain and the driver was overheard on his mobile phone saying, "I'm at 190 kmph and we're going to derail." HAL working in unison with the independent GPS would have warned the driver at a much earlier stage to reduce speed.

Control Rooms (Power Stations)

53. HAL monitors critical parameters

Any control room where serious overloads could be damaging to people, infrastructure or the environment would benefit from an extra layer of protection using the HAL/PSS human/computer analytical backstop.

Automatic Cars

54. Driverless cars will need backup

How far can we trust our fully automated cars in the near future? Recently, I was driving at night on a fast moving highway in foul weather with the rain lashing down, severely reducing visibility. How well will the automatics work in these conditions? My parking sensors were sounding randomly due to the intensity of the rain — I hope the fully automatic system will know not to jam on the brakes! Maybe here we could benefit from one extra layer of analysis?

Scientific Research

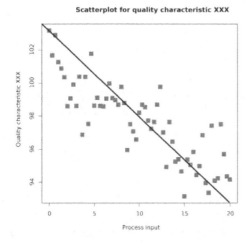

55. HAL looks for the desired result

Where a scientific experiment is running for purposes of research, a detector may be outputting data to a screen as in the example above. It may be more beneficial for the researchers to use HAL/PSS as a separate programming tool to look for the desired result rather than trying to add extra code to an older computer running alongside the detector. There could be an arrangement where several inputs are connected to one monitoring screen and now we only need to program HAL to look for the specific combinations required. Notifications would be sent to indicate progress as well as success. Minimal reprogramming would then be required to set up HAL to monitor a completely different experiment.

Air Traffic Control

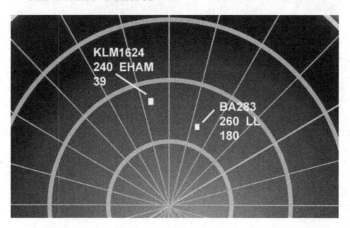

56. Air Traffic Control radar shows one aircraft at 24,000ft and another close at 26,000ft

Secondary radar returns contain data pertaining to each aircraft in the sector being controlled by the Air Traffic Controller. An example would be the aircraft's altitude display which is obviously vital for other traffic crossing in the area. HAL/PSS would again be an ideal addition to further enhance safety.

Mission to Mars

The next mission to Mars at time of writing is scheduled for the summer of 2020. It will be a rover mission, part of NASA's Mars Exploration Program. The mission also provides opportunities to gather knowledge and demonstrate technologies that address the challenges of future human expeditions to Mars. These include testing a method for producing oxygen from the Martian atmosphere, identifying other resources (such as subsurface water), improving landing techniques, and characterizing weather, dust, and other potential environmental conditions that could affect future astronauts living and working on Mars.

It looks like it won't be long before humans will be setting off for Mars. Due to the vulnerability of the mission, they could do with some of that computer technology that was available to Dave and his crew in *2001: A Space Odyssey*.

As a preamble, I would like to look at a bit of design philosophy that took people by surprise when webcams were first introduced. Most laptop computers have a small webcam sitting on top of the lid and next to it is a little light to inform you that the camera is running. Then it was discovered that some rogue software could secretly switch on your camera, bypassing the warning light, to expose your privacy or even your credit card details. We were all led to believe that the light only came on when the camera was working, but in fact the initial design flaw allowed for 2 distinctly separate functions. It could switch on the camera and then as an additional function it could switch on the light. But it should have been designed in series so that the software could only switch on the camera and then once the camera was activated, another independent circuit would switch on the light.

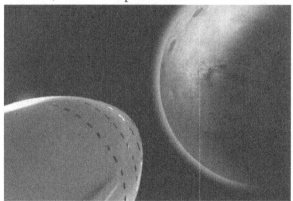

57. Space travel will necessitate total trust of onboard systems

This, too, is where things started to go wrong with HAL 2001 — in the design phase. HAL had complete autonomy of the spaceship and was able to come up with an excuse to persuade the astronauts to undergo an unnecessary Extravehicular Activity (EVA). A component needed changing as it was, according to HAL, going to fail catastrophically in 72 hours. Like the laptop camera, HAL could effectively cheat the system in order to get his own way, albeit for his own genuine reasons. The initial design needed to ensure that each conclusion reached by HAL went through a "virtual synapse." This would be accomplished by forcing HAL to output (hard wiring) his conclusion onto a screen. So the words "Antenna unit" would be displayed for our HAL/PSS to pick up and process. If anything untoward was brought to the attention of the crew by HAL 2001, they would do what I would do on a 747 if we needed to shutdown an engine. I would ask the first officer to "confirm." This is to check I had my hand on the correct engine shutdown lever before I potentially switched off the wrong engine.

So Dave would have asked HAL/PSS to "confirm Antenna unit." If the defect were genuine then the message would be forced out of HAL 2001 onto the screen and registered by PSS. But if the words were not registered, then we have a discrepancy and Mission Control would be automatically alerted. HAL 2001 wouldn't have been able to suppress the "Antenna unit" message as the architecture of the system would adopt the newly revised logic of the laptop webcam whereby there is now no direct connection to the webcam light.

The same would happen when Dave was outside of the spaceship and HAL switched off the life support system for the remaining hibernating crew. HAL/PSS would monitor the screen for any critical failure messages coming from the computer running the hibernation pods and independently alert the crew or Mission Control.

Thought provokingly, we observe in the film that HAL 2001 identified the reason for the false mechanical breakdown, as "human error" on the part of the designers in Urbana, Illinois where the computer was manufactured He also goes on to announce that the "mission was too important for human crew to jeopardize" and we see the final conflict of interests is settled when Dave breaks into the "Logic Memory Sensors" compartment and starts disconnecting HAL's memory chips.

Of course we are a long way off having such a sophisticated onboard computer such as HAL 2001 and so the realistic application of HAL/PSS would only be in line with the Heavy Aircrew Logic discussed in connection with aviation. It would specifically be useful as a monitoring tool on the eight month flight to Mars where the small crew will not be able to, so effectively, monitor the ship's systems for those massively extended periods compared to a mere 14 hour earth flight from Singapore to London.

CHAPTER 10: ACHIEVING 2001

What you can be certain of, as well as the existence of government depart-ments working out how to impose a breathing tax, is that there are various airliners flying around today on proving flights with pilots aboard that are only there as a backup in case the full automation fails. Such airliners will taxi out, take off and land on their own and could be referred to as "manned drones." There is an inevitable movement towards a pilotless flight deck, primarily to cut costs and increase efficiency, which is theoretically achiev-able because computers don't get tired. We know that drones have been very successful in operating missions especially in the Middle East and Afghani-stan. Well, we know they have successfully eliminated known targets, but what do we know about the track record of serviceability and reliability? How many have crashed on takeoff or landing or perhaps gone walk-about whilst on a mission?

I wonder whether any of the proving flights are using a 737 Max 8? Prob-ably not as they are still all grounded at time of writing and senior executives are answering questions on what appears to be a premature certification of an inherent design flaw. I live not too far from Farnborough Airport, where Sir Frank Whittle first came up with the idea of the jet engine. That was the easy part. Now he had to persuade the UK Ministry of Defence to agree it was not only a good idea but also that funding should be forthcoming for the research and development. The pressures on Sir Frank were more financial rather than a time race to complete the project but everyone obviously wants the development process to be completed as soon as possible and so there is always pressure on the timetable. The predecessor to the 737 Max 8, the

737-800 was the 8th generation of the most successful airliner ever built but technology had caught up with it and demanded some changes.

When the Boeing 737-100 first rolled out in 1967, the engines were fitted beneath the wings, as they are today, one on either side, and with the maximum thrust available at the time, there were no odd handling characteristics of the aircraft. As time progressed, noise became an important consideration, and soon engines were being designed with large fans at the front to significantly reduce the noise footprint, with only about half the air passing through the noisy jet engine.

58/59. 737-400 engine and pylon redesign on the Boeing 737-Max 8

However, a redesign was required as the now larger fan wouldn't fit under the wing anymore. So they squashed the engine to accommodate the 737-400 (first image above). As time went on, the fuselage length increased from about 28 meters to around 40 meters, and eventually it became necessary to increase the engine size to provide an overall better operating performance for the airlines.

It was decided to change the design of the pylons that attach the engine to the wing, so that a larger engine could be fitted, protruding further forward than before (second image above). This, though, had a side effect that caused the aircraft to pitch up into a potential stall when large amounts of this extra power were applied. To fix this, the designers added another computerized system called MCAS (Maneuvering Characteristics Augmentation System) to push the nose down when a vane on the outside of the aircraft detected a severe angle of attack. This extra layer of computerization is what I mean by another layer onto the "House of Cards." If the stall warning vane gets iced over or is damaged by a bird strike or knocked into by a maintenance vehicle on the apron, it will provide confusing data to the "series" computer system. In the two fatal accidents that grounded the aircraft, it appears the stall warning vane failed, feeding false information to the MCAS system and the autopilot automatically lowered the nose believing that there was an imminent stall situation — a series computer, knee-jerk reaction.

The MCAS system only activates when the flaps are in the up position so when the crews retracted the flaps after takeoff, the computer took over to force the nose down. Various modifications will now need to be made to the 737 Max 8 but as the loss of elevator control is an extremely serious situation, the fix needs to ensure that any stabilizer runaway situation is identified as soon as possible and the crew offered all assistance to deal with the problem. As this book is dealing with improved safety, I will make two points about the 737 Max 8 situation.

Firstly, could HAL/PSS have helped had it been fitted? Pitch in an aircraft is controlled by the tailplane stabilizer and the elevators. The tailplane stabilizer does all the heavy lifting and can be thought of as a mini-wing at the back of the fuselage. It has to be set at the required angle into the slipstream and balances all the pitch up/down forces so the pilot doesn't need to pull or push with great force to keep the aircraft level. The elevators on the rear of the tailplane stabilizer allow the pilot to make fine pitch movements to accurately keep the aircraft on the correct angle of climb or descent and in no way can overpower the tailplane stabilizer. The angular position of this mini-wing is critical in any stage of flight so if it is involved in a "runaway" on its own, the pilots need to be able to switch it off and so Boeing has 2 cut-out switches which stop its movement. The pilots then have to go through a process of manually winding the trim system to recover the aircraft — which can be quite difficult — especially at high speed. If the pitch trim information were available on the pilot flight displays, HAL/PSS could now see this trim position and together with the artificial horizon reading, could ascertain whether the vane is working properly. As well as warning of excessive stabilizer trim movement, another message would remind the crew to extend the flaps to cancel the MCAS. Now the stabilizer should be available for normal operation.

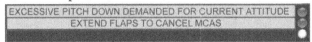

Secondly, was the 737 Max 8 with its inherent fault and MCAS fix introduced too quickly in our hurry to advance (for whatever reason) and are there any other combinations we need to consider before relentlessly pressing ahead with full automation? The reason I included the earlier chapter on "Thinking Computers," and how they work down at the fundamental level, was to expose the underlying simplicity of the workings as a magician's trick rather than a significant step towards our understanding of the human thought process. I really doubt that the computers we have today are going to give us the insight we need to understand the innermost workings of the human brain. I believe that quantum computing will possibly provide the first step in this direction and therefore I will concede that the Babbage system we currently use will at least have been responsible for getting us to the necessary starting blocks for full automation. Why quantum? Because quantum is associated with our parallel logic as it contains three states, not just the two we use in binary, 1 and 0. The third state is a 1/0 or a combination of On and Off (in quantum language, a qubit). Like a tossed coin in midair, it is both heads and tails at the same time and is considered as its undefined property before the final answer is revealed when it settles on the floor. These superpositions can be entangled with those of other objects, meaning their final outcomes will be mathematically related even if we don't yet know what they are. So effectively an entire branch of related calculations is done for us behind the scenes (parallel processing) instead of having to wait for our current pinch point processor to go through them one by one.

As we have said, it's maybe time to evolve a different type of design methodology for the future to include a "checks and balances" system to operate alongside series computers and human brains to provide maximum coverage of the "cheese holes" until such a time we manage to open up Schrödinger's box and peer into the mysterious world of quantum. Meanwhile, there's another problem we need to overcome.

Asimov

Isaac Asimov came up with a set of rules to govern the behavior of robots that were designed specifically to have a degree of autonomy. He wrote these rules in the 1940s because, as he had a human brain, he was able to predict that there was going to be a potential problem. Now that we are really getting to grips with Artificial Intelligence, these laws are more relevant than ever; and even back in 1968 Arthur C. Clarke saw the dangers and potential traps.

- First Law — A robot may not injure a human being or, through inaction, allow a human being to come to harm.
- Second Law — A robot must obey the orders given it by human beings except where such orders would conflict with the First Law.
- Third Law — A robot must protect its own existence as long as such protection does not conflict with the First or Second Laws.

There is genuine concern that one day robots may overpower mankind and take over the world. Although this might appear to be a very futuristic problem, the closest we have got so far is with military drones. When a target is identified and a decision is made to fire a missile, as I understand it, the operative flying the drone in their bunker will now switch to automatic mode and detach completely from the operation. This way she no longer can be held responsible for the act of killing, especially when innocent bystanders are involved. However, it does somewhat conflict with Asimov's rules but of course, Asimov isn't one of today's world leaders.

HAL/PSS would allow a second set of rules to apply internally within the robot to control any of these excessive behaviors that may have been learned through machine learning. We discussed earlier the process of back-propagation when we were working out how to recognize a printed number as a 5 or a 7. If the "weights" were maliciously altered, the backpropagation would eventually reinforce the Artificial Intelligence elements of the robot and there would be nothing to uphold Asimov's laws — the robots could dominate.

This is a definition of backpropagation I found on-line and I have added the label *Computer* to differentiate it from how a *human* and *HAL/PSS* would see it.

- *Computer:* "Backpropagation is the essence of neural net training. It is the practice of fine-tuning the weights of a neural net based on the error rate (i.e. loss) obtained in the previous epoch (i.e. iteration). Proper tuning of the weights ensures lower error rates, making the model reliable by increasing its generalization."

- *Human:* Backpropagation could result in the process being manipulated by a fellow human who I have evolved to mistrust, through backpropagation into world history.

- *HAL/PSS:* Backpropagation and robot operation will be monitored for specific human abuses utilizing a human referencing system that will act as a regulator for the robot.

This could resist abuses but now comes the hard bit — getting all nations to agree a protocol; although if it were not followed by an individual nation then it could be seen by others as the equivalent of stockpiling for war.

In chapter 3, we were discussing how a robot might be able to make a cup of coffee if it were suitably equiped with arms and mechanical hands, but where are they? I was led to believe that by the year 2020, at least, these machines would be making my dinner, doing the housework and covering all those menial tasks around the home. Again, as with AI computers today, these machines can do various individual tasks very well but the problem comes when we attempt universal integration with the 'real' world. The issue is not with universal integration, it is with the interpretation of what we mean by 'real' world. What part of the real world do our brains interact with? Is it connected with the science of how atoms interact with one another or how quantum entangles the very same particles or is it in association with the spare dimensions predicted by quantum theory or could it be linked to dark matter interactions or maybe another whole branch of science that only exists in a singularity at the centre of a black hole?

All of these concepts are merely interpretations by our own human brain that is itself encapsulated within an enigmatic universe that we just don't understand. So the point I am making is that it is some expectation for us to build a machine that is as good as the most complex entity of all time, which has itself evolved from nothing, inside a universe that we just cannot comprehend. Practically speaking, this is what we will need to do in order to realize the dream of fully robotic servants that seamlessly interact with us, within our world. I'm not saying we or a future species will never get close but I am reasoning for us to manage our expectations to be within realistic limits.

MH 370 Ironies

The mystery of Malaysian flight MH370 has still not been solved as of July 2020, and until we locate the aircraft we will probably never know what actually happened. However, we can piece together quite a bit from the supposed evidence we have so far.

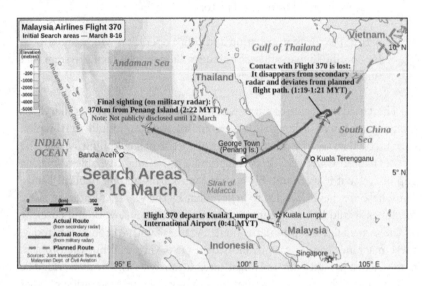

60. MH370 last reported route before disappearing

The Boeing 777 took off from Kuala Lumpur at 12:41 a.m. local time on the 8th March 2014 carrying 227 passengers and 12 crew members. It headed north east towards Ho Chi Minh City on its way to its destination, Beijing (dashed route above).

When over the South China Sea and at an Air Traffic Control border (FIR boundary), the aircraft apparently turned hard left and flew almost exactly down the FIR (Flight Information Region) boundary between Malaysia and Thailand. The turn was so quick it is estimated that the autopilot must have been disengaged so the angle of bank could be increased to well above the normal angle. The transponder and ACARS were then switched off and it supposedly headed for the island of Penang, after which it turned north-westerly out to sea (solid route above). Once out of radar coverage, the 777 disappeared. A lot has been written about the incident, so what are the possible scenarios?

- The aircraft was hijacked for political motives or for the hijacker(s) to seek asylum in another country, but they got lost and crashed into the sea after exhausting the fuel, 7 hours later.

- The aircraft was hijacked and shot down by one of the governments involved. But in this case the wreckage would have been hard to conceal.
- The flight was hijacked by one of the pilots or crew on a suicide mission.
- The aircraft was hijacked by remote control from a laptop computer onboard or from a ground station.

Looking at what we have been given, it would be hard to accept that the chosen point of route divergence at the FIR boundary in the South China Sea was a coincidence. It appears to have been selected because it is the point at which there is an ATC cone of silence, where the aircraft is out of radio range from both Kuala Lumpur and Ho Chi Minh City control for about 10 minutes. The aircraft then happens to fly along the FIR boundary between Malaysia and Thailand. It also seems that the authorities were not particularly interested in there being a 777 airliner rampaging on the loose, post 9/11, within a stone's throw of Bangkok and Kuala Lumpur, as apparently no military jet fighters were scrambled. There was also a 4 hour delay before any authority was notified about the rogue aircraft and very strangely, neither authority could pass on data about the precise track and altitudes the aircraft took whilst threatening their airspace. From other evidence that has come to light since, it is also suggested that the aircraft flew a specific offset (used by professional pilots) whilst heading away from Penang, to maneuver the aircraft away from the busy airway, avoiding other on-coming flights, before making a turn heading south and disappearing.

From the scenarios given above, it would appear that the only thing for sure is that the aircraft was hijacked, whether by passengers, crew or remotely by external interference. A well briefed but amateur pilot hijacker could very well have taken over the flight deck and switched off the Transponder and ACARS. But some time later in the proceedings, it appears the aircraft is the hands of a professional pilot who knows about offsets. Why would a criminal hijacker go to the trouble of dodging other aircraft? They would either be actually trying to cause a collision or would have made a beeline for their objective, say the Petronas towers. The TCAS system (Traffic Alert and Collision Avoidance System) onboard all the other aircraft in the area would have taken care of any mid-air collision risk, so it is curious as to why such care was taken with the offset. Anyway, we can only speculate and until we find the aircraft we may never know.

But it does raise an interesting question. After 9/11, many people asked why the U.S. military jet fighters weren't launched sooner. The answer, I would suggest, is because this was a "real world" situation, not a Hollywood fantasy. To react so rapidly without gathering sufficient intelligence would have been practically impossible. But to launch none at all to investigate MH370?

People also asked what could be done to prevent 9/11 happening again. Is the idea of remotely controlled airliners that bizarre? Is it even possible and would it be accepted by professional pilots and the travelling public if a hijacked airliner was remotely controlled by the military? Well, it is certainly possible; we are all familiar with unmanned drones flying around, some with missiles attached. We also know that Boeing has developed the MQ-25 unmanned aircraft for US carriers. As they state, "the MQ-25 will provide the needed robust refueling capability thereby extending the combat range of deployed Boeing F/A-18 Super Hornet, Boeing EA-18G Growler, and Lockheed Martin F-35C fighters."

61. Boeing's MQ-25 **Unmanned Aerial Vehicle**

Boeing's MQ-25 is up and running and interestingly, the USAF trained more UAV (Unmanned Aerial Vehicle) pilots in 2012 than ordinary jet fighter pilots for the first time.

Can this remote control ability be installed into a civil airliner?

When any modern civil airliner is being flown through the autopilot system, all the operational commands are routed from the flight deck to the electronics bay, under the fuselage floor, which then enacts the command whether it be to turn the aircraft or to lock on to an ILS landing beam. Without getting into this too deeply, I am satisfied that it is certainly possible and the existence of the MQ-25 sort of proves the point.

The second question is more complex — would it be accepted by professional pilots and the travelling public? I don't think it would be accepted at all on any grounds... apart from... the extremis of the 9/11 situation. Imagine if a military ground based pilot could be efficiently switched in by the Air Traffic Control unit that is handling the hijack situation. ATC know the identification of the aircraft which would be linked to a computer holding all the specific data for that particular aircraft. So a ground based pilot could take control in just a few minutes. With complete worldwide coverage using communication satellites, no aircraft would ever be out of range. Through predetermined protocols, the aircraft systems would be isolated from the hijacker and the aircraft could be directed to a military airfield for an automatic landing. I would suggest that most governments around the world would agree that such a solution in extremis would be better than allowing an airliner to be used as an ICBM (Intercontinental Ballistic Missile) against them and the general public.

Sounds good, but of course there are many problems. Even if you override specific controls inside the flight deck, the hijacker could shut down the engines, unless you override that specific engine control system. Now we are hoping that the override system doesn't go wrong or get hacked into during a regular flight! You would start by triggering a disconnect switch in the avionics bay so the Heading switch in the flight deck is disabled. You would also ensure that the autopilot cannot now be disconnected in the normal way so the would-be hijacker can no longer control the heading of the aircraft. This would be easily accomplished at the autopilot control box under the floor where all autopilot disconnect signals routed from the flight deck would be intercepted by a switching unit. If this switching unit were to become stuck during a regular flight, the flight crew, cooperating with the ground agency, would carry out an Autoland and nobody would be any the wiser. In a hijack, through satellite link, the ground based pilot would control the heading of the aircraft and just by removing this one function, the threat would be severely diminished. Although the hijacker could crash the aircraft, his target and objective would be forever shrouded in mystery and the much sought after publicity denied. But what about the fate of the passengers and crew?

So the irony is that one of the far-fetched suggestions of what could have caused the disappearance of MH370 is something we may need to contemplate to help disincentivize terrorists from hijacking our civil airlines in the first place. They would now have to face the fact that they will always lose control of the situation. It's possible that the ground controller could steer the aircraft to make a safe automatic landing at the nearest suitable airfield but here we run into the same old problem. If we stack up the House of Cards with increased sophistication in the aircraft series computers, we are asking for unexpected failures during normal operations which would defeat the object. A difficult problem to solve but by having a quasi-intelligent flight deck door, it may go towards solving this issue. Finally, when considering the fate of MH370, it certainly makes sense for the HAL system to be "texting" its latitude and longitude every ten minutes or so. This would be easily accomplished and would have provided essential data for the Search and Rescue teams, ensuring they were guided to the correct crash site. It was such a pity that they only received data from one satellite, which resulted in there being only one massive search area. Had the aircraft's data been shared with just one other satellite, the search area would have been manageable and the mystery would probably have been solved.

The Space Shuttle disasters also show up a separate problem for the future of fully automated systems. When there are unlimited funds flowing into a beloved, ground breaking project, the attention to detail is so intense that we normally manage to survive the early introductory phase without loss of life, at least to the astronauts. But when the operations become the norm, we tend to take our eye off the ball. The problem is that there are thousands of different combinations available out there for things to go wrong and they are all waiting in probabilistic order to put in an unwanted appearance. This means that the most likely things to go wrong have already been pre-designed into the system and now it's just a question of being alert to the awkward combinations (Murphy's law) that cannot possibly be considered at the design stage as they are so numerous.

The weather is around us, every day, knocking at the door trying to take a piece out of whatever machines we create, and corrosive elements work in unison to provide perfect conditions for Murphy's law to flourish. The more sophisticated our systems, the more elements there are to go wrong or degrade, and it seems this will be a never ending battle.

Air France 447 would probably not have happened in the 1970s, operated by a 747 Classic (747-100). It's only because we have greater sophistication that this type of accident has worked its way up the probabilistic order. Immediately, we again have to point out that many, many other types of accident have been avoided by this greater computer sophistication but the argument here is how we improve the statistics and I don't believe a move to full automation is credible yet.

What's happening in the depths of the under floor computer processor is irrelevant, it is only what is being presented in an intelligible form to the human pilots that is important in an emergency and to help sort this information we need a further partnership, not more layers of technology and responsibility built into the series computer system. On a flight I was operating from Los Angeles to Heathrow, the underfloor computer processor was doing a grand job keeping the 747-400 straight and level and flying at the correct speed — until we started to cross the Rockies near Las Vegas.

We had encountered mountain waves, whereby the Rockies had set off a sine wave shaped disturbance in the airflow and instead of coming straight at us, the airflow was partly coming at us from above which had the effect of forcing the aircraft downwards. To counteract this, the autopilot raised the nose to try and stay level and the auto thrust increased to maximum power for that altitude. But when mountain waves are strong, it is impossible for the aircraft to maintain level flight and target speed — something has to give. So although the power was increased, the speed started to drift back towards the stall point. What to do?

Automatics: "I don't know what you are talking about — I will notify you with a stall warning claxon when we approach critical low speed."

Flight Crew: "Looks like mountain waves, suggest you (First Officer) call Air Traffic Control and tell them we need to descend, I'll use the autopilot to start a 5 degree banked turn before the speed reduces to a point where any banked turn could precipitate an early stall. The turn will take us to the edge of the airway and out of the path of any oncoming aircraft below us, so if I have to descend without ATC permission, we can do so safely. We should also monitor the TCAS system, until we have good contact with ATC."

As it was, ATC gave us an immediate descent and there was no incident. Furthermore, the warning was sent back along the airway over the radio to aircraft on the same route whose pilots could now plan a strategy. TCAS (Traffic Collision Avoidance System) is a system that displays the position and relative altitude of any aircraft in the vicinity to avoid a mid-air collision. The travelling public don't always connect with the vulnerability of flying until, of course, something goes wrong. If everything is working well onboard, then fine, but our business is about when it's not working so well, and it sometimes requires high levels of awareness and problem solving abilities that present day computers cannot emulate.

Serious mountain wave encounters are relatively rare, but cumulonimbus clouds (CB) are responsible for about 100 lightning strikes to the Earth's surface... every second. That's about 8 million per day and 3 billion each year. CBs can grow to levels that civilian aircraft cannot rise above; and so they must be avoided by flying around them, sometimes meaning up to a 100-mile detour. Jet streams high in the atmosphere can cause severe turbulence and so decisions have to be made about lateral route deviations and vertical flight level changes, not only for the comfort of passengers and crew but ultimately for their safety. These deviations have to be coordinated with Air Traffic

Control, and with the ever increasing amount of commercial flights in the skies, if we are to solely rely on computers, we need to consider the Kessler syndrome.

Kessler proposed that one small collision of man-made objects in low earth orbit could cause a cascade in which each collision would generate more space debris that would further increase the likelihood of further collisions, finally bringing down the entire satellite network. How well will the ATC system cope with thousands of requests from automated aircraft to avoid CBs? Do ATC take on the responsibility to allow a deviation and if they can't due to vast amounts of traffic in the area, do they take responsibility for the possible onboard injuries sustained in the ensuing severe turbulence? Sure you can show me how a test aircraft can detect a thunderstorm and fly around it but we need to be realistic with our expectations when the numbers get unmanageably large during monsoon season, for example.

Although the report has not yet been published at time of writing, there were rumors of a lightning strike as a possible cause of the Sukhoi Superjet-100 accident in Moscow on 5 May 2019. The aircraft appears to have suffered what was described as an electrical failure after takeoff. It returned to Moscow–Sheremetyevo airport, where it crashed on landing, bursting into flames. The poor handling of the final approach and landing may have been pilot error, but it did look like there were control issues which led to the heavy touchdown. Without speculating before the report is published, it still remains a problem for a fully automated aircraft to guarantee isolation from a bad lightning strike. As I mentioned in a previous chapter, when flying into Islamabad, a lightning strike tore a 2 ft by 2ft hole in the underside of the 747 Classic wing we were flying — what would happen if it struck near the electronics bay on a current modern airliner or worse still, a future fully automated airliner?

Another tragic incident has just occurred in Iran where all onboard were lost when it appears the Iranian military mistakenly shot down a Ukraine International Airlines (UIA) flight departing from Tehran International airport. In line with the theme we are discussing, I wonder what level of automation was inherent in the missile firing system. I, of course, will never know but it does raise the question of possible vulnerabilities in automatic systems, especially when they have the potential of making such dire mistakes.

Experience can be very different from doing a lot of what you normally do. You wouldn't expect an experienced pilot to never have undergone an engine failure. But most airline pilots have never experienced a real engine failure on a regular flight carrying passengers, mainly due to regulation, intelligent design and the incredibly high standards of our ground engineers. All of this practice is done in simulators, twice yearly, together with other types of failure that could cause serious issues, like flap and undercarriage malfunctions. No one person is responsible for the very high standards of safety that we all enjoy in aviation today, it has been build brick by brick over the years and sadly some of the greatest advances have only followed after the analysis of serious accidents. The founder of the theory of gravity (the pilot's nemesis) wrote in a letter, "If I had seen further than other men, it is by standing on the shoulders of giants." This is the truth of how any industry evolves and today's pilots are no exception, being just as good as any other era of airmen. It is even arguable that they are better, in the sense that they have been able to learn from all that has gone before, as Sir Isaac far too modestly alluded to in his letter. And this is where another problem comes as we face the dawn of full automation.

How do we keep our pilots at the high standards we enjoy today whilst the onset of futuristic automation keeps them at arm's length? The more the automatics fly the aircraft, the less practice is afforded to the crews. It may be only after a catastrophic failure that the pilot will be called upon to use his upmost skills that have been steadily eroded over time. It's the same with any computerized system that fails. Look at how bad it gets when the airline check-in computer goes down. Thank goodness someone remembered the procedure from days gone by, pre-computers with handwritten lists and manual loadsheets. The worst thing that's going to happen is a horrendous ATC delay, but what if we need to fall back to basics following a systems malfunction in an aircraft that the crew has flown automatically for the last 3 months. And then, of course, I am assuming that at some stage the plan will be for there only to be one pilot onboard — interesting.

This thought brings us to the question, "Are we going to have any choice in the future whether we fly on an autonomous airliner?" Will we be forced to board a pilotless, fully automatic aircraft if we need to travel long distances? An academic paper has recently been published in the *Journal of Aviation, Aeronautics and Aerospace* entitled "Autonomous Airliners Anytime Soon?" by Vance, Bird and Tiffin (Embry-Riddle Aeronautical University Oklahoma State University 2019). The main premise of the article is to collate all the surveyed data from the public to statistically calculate when in the future there is likely to be a greater than 50% acceptance to fly without pilots. There are a lot of famous sayings about statistics and the report takes us into detailed mathematical projections of public sentiment but the bottom line is that today 30% of Americans would board a pilotless aircraft and that 50% would be prepared to do so by the year 2030. The idea is that once we have reached the 50% mark, it will provide the green light for the mass roll out and development of autonomous airliners. The report also states that 78% of the public supported a fully autonomous airliner if one backup pilot was onboard. This is one step down from the current situation where 100% of the public support an autonomous airliner if two backup pilots are onboard!

At the end of the report there are the normal references that were cited to add credence to the article. I have found another one to ponder over. It is by The Gambling Commission, entitled "Gambling participation in 2018: Behavior, awareness and attitudes Annual Report," published in February 2019. The stand-out statistics are:

- 32% of the respondents have participated in gambling in the past four weeks, excluding those who had only played the National Lottery draws.
- 30% of the respondents think that gambling is fair and can be trusted.

No problem with gambling if you choose to do it — but not with my money, if you don't mind.

Now you have the target date of 2030 confirmed, do you feel ready to cast your vote, or would you be seeking a bit more information? We have to put aside the cash benefits for interested companies and the ticket discount promises to passengers as, from a professional perspective, these are totally irrelevant to the pure argument. I think the answer to the "Autonomous Airliners Anytime Soon?" question is, "Only when we are ready." In other words, have we evolved our systems sufficiently to seamlessly move from the old into the new without a ghastly collapse midway? I would suggest that the first thing to do is to drastically reduce the current accident rate and yes, certainly by incorporating the very latest AI computers but in unison with the extremely successful model we have today. If Air France 447 was to happen again and the brand new AI computer goes on to save the day, handing back control to the pilots, then fine. If Qantas flight 72, where the uncommanded pitch-down maneuver injured several passengers, prevented itself from thumping the control wheel forward and instead informed the crew of a necessary autopilot disconnect, then fine. At this point you may have my vote but we need to think this through carefully and discard the natural impatience we may suffer when, say, planning to build a bridge across a river.

We want to get to the other side for provisions but want to do so cheaply and quickly. There is no actual need for extra provisions but we are planning ahead. Do we build a weak bridge quickly that could collapse into the river, having to accept many crossings with small cartloads or do we build a strong bridge slowly and make fewer crossings with much larger cartloads and reduced risk of collapse? This, to me, is the dilemma we are facing today with full automation. The series style of thought says, "Let's just build the bridge starting right now to accomplish the task." But with no need for provisions, we might be better off by considering all parallel factors and consequences to build the stronger bridge. Either way a bridge is going to be built but we *must* control the race.

The Embry-Riddle report did make me smile a couple of times. To set the scene, the authors open with a businessman arriving at the airport worried about possible delays to his flight. The stewardess says, quote, "Oh, we're ready to go...this flight is now totally automated!" My mind flashes back to good old regular ops when I used to board my aircraft, and accordingly I imagine the more realistic scenario where the futuristic engineer comes on scene to say that the flight is going to be delayed because there is a fault with the FITCS (Fully Integrated Thrust Computer System). "I've tried 50 times but I can't cancel the warning light," he says. I further imagine the aircraft dispatcher asking if she should call out some pilots. "Yes," replies the engineer, "We could get some pilots but there aren't any bloody throttles on this one!" If we build the House of Cards higher with extra layers of the fictitious FITCS, we only increase the chance for something to go wrong which in turn means a greater likelihood of delays. Remember, many of the other regular scenarios won't have gone away. Weather problems, like high crosswinds, will still be in the mix and initially, there will need to be more limiting restrictions applied, leading to even greater delays.

Smile number two was that the report had been subject to the rigors of our 21st century computerized spell checker systems, except that there was a spelling mistake in the title of one of the graphics, "Price Effect on Willingess to Fly." Pedantic, you can call me, but that's only permissible because you have a parallel wired brain that can easily see that the word should have been "Willingness." You also realize that there are no other realistic interpretations and there are no consequences of using this incorrect data. Furthermore, you will be able to empathize with the mistake, knowing we have all made these sorts of errors before and therefore will think no less of the academic argument contained within. That is, you will have the ability to *ignore* the error. The computer can do none of these things, and although it is reasonably good at spell checking, it just can't understand the graphical representation of a word unless it is specifically told to load up a separate program. The problem is that, what seems pedantic to you and me could be fatal in an automatic airliner, especially after a computer software update. So not a good advertisement for the "no humans necessary" argument.

A quick thought about what we actually mean by automation? We can easily see how a machine can replace a person, say, cutting wheat in a field. But does it replace the farmer? When pilots flew aircraft before autopilots, they were metaphorically juggling about 5 balls — aircraft control, navigation, communication, systems monitoring etc. The advent of autopilots meant that one of the balls was now being handled by the automatics. As time went on with improved systems, the pilot only had to juggle one ball, throwing it up and catching it — seems like they may soon be redundant! The reason for this thought sequence is because we perceive automation as linked to replacement, but if you were to look into a flight deck today, you would still see all 5 balls being tossed into the air. They haven't disappeared, it's all still real and happening, you are still in an airplane at 39,000 ft, just as vulnerable as you always were. The navigation computer is juggling its ball and synchronizing it with the autopilot ball, overseen by the pilots who will catch one or both of the balls if necessary. All pilots have had times when they have been forced to revert to the 3 ball juggle and as we have seen, some have taken on 6 to rescue serious emergencies. So flight deck "automation" shouldn't translate to redundancy, it should translate to assistance or cooperation.

The Embry-Riddle report ended by considering a possible way forward. Should we license the already existing unmanned cargo drones and aircraft fitted with full automation to fly pilotlessly amongst regular passenger flights to develop the technology? So this is the introduction to what I hope will be the widely accepted best practice for our times concerning this difficult debate. Yes, but openly monitored by a board of international professionals ranging from national authorities (CAA, FAA etc.) to pilots, engineers and other aviation specialists in conjunction with the technological and developmental companies. We cannot afford to take one big leap at this stage and should participate in a steady but gradual evolution, with the primary aim of greater passenger safety. Aviation is a truly global industry and what one country or large organization decides to do should not adversely affect other countries until the necessary due diligence has been completed. HAL would be a perfect fit for this as it works in parallel with the newly evolving systems but at the same time enhancing the link between man and machine. If not HAL then some other "out of the box" thinking needs to be done whilst we wait for quantum computers to come onboard. Once we have achieved that much improved level of safety, far more than we have today, we can start to remove that necessary interface between man and machine and only then will we be able to convince the travelling public, especially considering the 2018/9 statistics.

I think the most important analogy of all is the one that takes us back to biology. The *medulla oblongata* is located in the brain stem which controls a number of involuntary functions such as when we take a breath. This is our autopilot, ensuring each breath is taken at the right time. Run up the stairs and the "breath autopilot" will increase the breath rate just as an aircraft autopilot will increase altitude if a climb is required. The *medulla oblongata* doesn't know why it has to change the breath rate, it just does it. It developed very early on in our evolution and is situated in the old part of the brain — the brain stem. The prefrontal cortex is located in the new part that evolved much later. Here, we not only understand *why* we breathe but also what we should do if there were an emergency, like pneumonia for instance. In this case the *medulla oblongata* will throw the doctors and nurses its juggling ball and wait for the patient to die. The prefrontal cortex, though, goes into "parallel mode" and uniquely takes in multiple pathway possibilities, justifying its evolutionary seat at the table. Not only can we introduce pure oxygen but we could also build a machine to ventilate the patient and then there'll be a ton of other more subtle procedures that only the medically qualified will know about. Do doctors and surgeons make mistakes? Shall we start to replace them with AI computers? Would an AI computer have come up with the idea of a ventilator? Does an AI computer know what an "idea" is? Will future AI computers outsmart the prefrontal cortex when we face a newly evolved pathogen?

To help visualize the difficulties confronting the plane makers and the companies rushing to develop autonomous computer systems, the write-up below is a typical program that all pilots undergo for 8 hours over two days in simulators. In order to have our licenses revalidated, these exercises are necessary every six months and each time a different set of problems and failures are practiced. This is what might be covered during a 2 day check.

- Autopilot systems fault after takeoff requiring the pilot to take over control and recover from the stall.
- Fire in the cargo hold necessitating an immediate return to land with no time to dump fuel (normally necessary to reduce the aircraft weight to be within certified limits). The aircraft will be touching down at 207 miles per hour (about the top speed of a F1 racing car) and as a result will not be able to use the normal flap setting. Pilots are reminded that they cannot use the Autoland system as it has not been certified for use in these circumstances and may be unpredict-

able. After a manual landing, the captain has to decide on whether a passenger evacuation is required and, if so, initiates the command.

• Air Traffic Control make a mistake and steer the aircraft towards high ground — the pilots have to manually intervene and recover the situation when the automatic Ground Proximity Warning alerts them to the error.

• The crew have been warned of reported Windshear on short finals and have to decide whether to abandon the approach. As part of the exercise, the pilots are requested to continue the approach and end up with a full thrust Windshear Go-around maneuver and diversion. On landing the crew are encouraged to discuss whether an earlier decision to divert, based on the reports, would have been best.

• After an engine failure on takeoff, the crew have to decide whether to return for an immediate landing at the departure airfield which now has limiting crosswinds or divert elsewhere where there is good weather but very limited landing aids.

How will a fall-back, ground-based pilot deal with an Autopilot systems fault? Who decides to evacuate the aircraft after an emergency landing? How will a ground based pilot judge the severity of turbulence on short finals to land? Today's airline crews work closely together to solve all these problems so you can imagine how difficult it's going to be for a remote team of drone pilots or even an onboard super computer for that matter.

We have come a long, long way with aircraft design and systems but still suffer catastrophic accidents with the figurative collapse of the House of Cards. Airliner fatalities have been relatively few over the past 10 years but we need to be mindful of the "almost accidents" that could have ended up with fatalities had it not been for that most essential element of all — luck. If we want to protect ourselves from computer hackers, faulty pitot tube heaters or computer malpractice on the way to Jupiter, we could do with a third layer of protection before we attempt Automation-Max. We have seen why 3 INS systems are installed, why 3 Autoland computers are required and how both pilots and computers can individually fail. Even author Arthur C. Clarke realized the necessity of having humans onboard, in charge, and ensured that not everyone was hibernating for that long journey to Jupiter.

The travelling salesman problem asks the following question: "Given a list of cities and the distances between each pair of cities, what is the shortest possible route that visits each city and returns to the origin city?" This seems like a bread and butter problem for a computer but although it can estimate the answer fairly accurately, once the number of cities gets into the thousands, the pinch point in the series processor makes it practically impossible to calculate the correct answer. There are just too many loops to run through the hourglass pinch point and it becomes what is called an NP time problem (Nondeterministic Polynomial) or as most people know it as, impossible! Quantum computers may be able to solve these problems that seem to be impossible or would take a traditional computer an impractical amount of time (a billion years) to solve, but they are very fragile. Any kind of vibration impacts the atoms that quantum computers rely upon and causes what is called "decoherence" — so not good in an aircraft. Decoherence is the process in which a system's behavior changes from that which can be explained by quantum mechanics to that which can be explained by classical mechanics meaning the system loses all its hidden, related mathematical calculations.

One day this technology will come, I'm sure, and we'll be able to solve more than just the travelling salesman problem. Until then, we should not replace the all-important parallel system, namely the pilots. We should keep developing our series computers to help us operate the flight more effectively but we maybe should consider introducing a third element to try and eliminate those stubborn last few remaining holes in the cheese.

There will be much intense lobbying for the introduction of autonomous airliners into our skies as we approach the year 2030, perhaps even earlier. Hopefully we will adopt a cautious, controlled approach utilizing some of that Crew Resource Management thinking to build a robust system that can evolve at the right pace to ensure its longevity.

I can envisage the futuristic dream of aircraft manufacturers and airlines where the flight deck is replaced by two Ultra-First Class seats with the rather nice view of the world that pilots get to enjoy today. The aircraft would be flown automatically, overseen by a ground pilot controller and to entice passengers to get on such an aircraft there would be an onboard, under floor compartment at the front of the aircraft, much like a World War II bomb aimer position, from which, the passengers would be told, "*a member of staff will land the aircraft in the unlikely event of something going wrong.*" The plan would be for the Dispatcher at the airport to decide on how much fuel to load, board the passengers, oversee the refueling and loading and then ensure the auto-tug has robotically arrived at the nosewheel. Then the dispatcher would text the ground pilot controller to take over. Provided he isn't handling an emergency in the quota of flights for the day, the flight will be set to "auto pushback" once the Air Traffic Control computer is happy...

Well, "that's the way it's going" — isn't it?

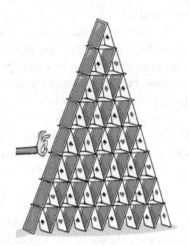

Thinking Computers

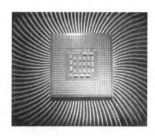

I want to discuss what is happening at the core of the computer processor. The central element is the transistor which is an On/Off switch. Here is a brief description of the functionality of a transistor, but it will not be necessary to probe into its detailed workings.

A transistor is fundamentally a flip-flop switch, much like a regular light switch on the wall. When you flick the light switch, electricity flows to the light bulb and the light comes on. The difference with a transistor is that instead of your finger flipping the switch, a clever arrangement in the transistor allows for a small electric current to do the physical switching. Once the transistor receives the small current, it flips the switch and importantly allows the switch to remain in that set position even when the small current is subsequently switched off. Moreover, a feedback system allows the transistor to know its last state, so if it was On, it now flips to Off and if it was Off, it flips to On.

Thus, when the ceiling light is On or the transistor is On, it is considered as a 1. When the ceiling light is Off or the transistor is Off, it is considered as a zero. Bearing in mind that the speed of electricity flow is extremely fast, we now have the capability to make many thousands of switches per second... and welcome to the Information Age.

This box is a representation of a transistor. It is empty, so is considered to be OFF or Value Zero.

This is a representation of a transistor set to ON.

A small electric current is used to switch the transistor On or OFF and it remains On or OFF until it is told otherwise. In the microprocessor there is a group of boxes or transistors like this shown below, laid out in a row: In our BBC computer there are 8 boxes. They are numbered right to left as this is the order in which they will be analyzed and processed.

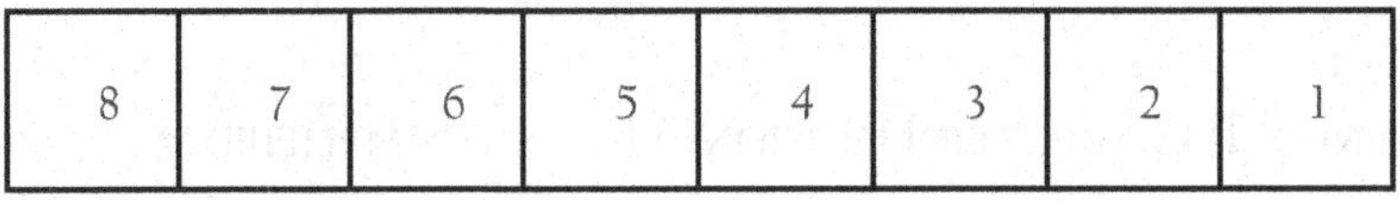

8	7	6	5	4	3	2	1

Here all 8 boxes are switched OFF, which means the boxes contain 00000000. This represents the number zero.

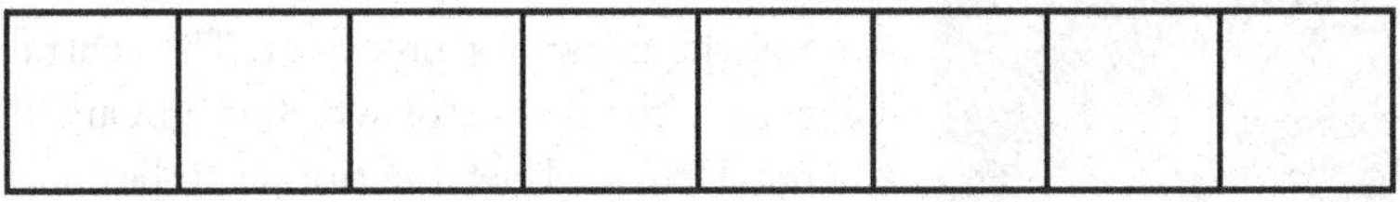

Now we will pass a small current through some of the boxes to cause them to SWITCH. Here 2 boxes are switched on and 6 are switched off, which means the boxes contain 00001010. This represents the number ten as will be shown below.

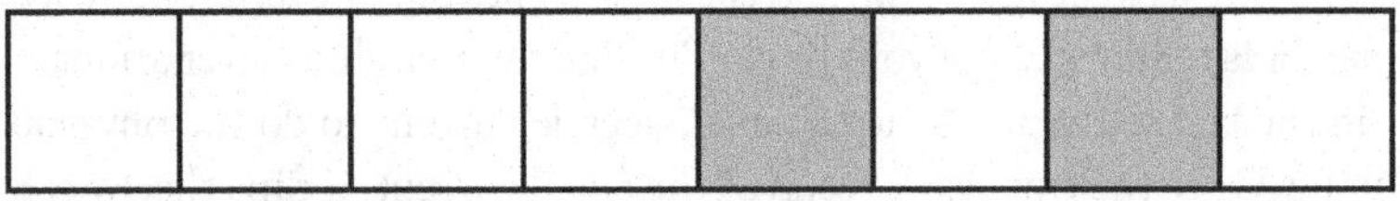

The numbering system works like this:

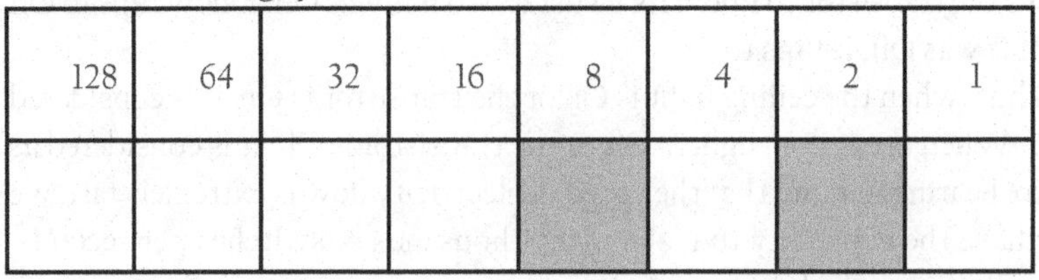

128	64	32	16	8	4	2	1

Far right is 1, then moving left the boxes represent increasing numbers. You may recognize this as the binary system, which works in exactly the same way as our decimal system except that when you reach 10 in our decimal system, you carry one and revert the units to zero. In binary when you reach 2, you carry one and revert the units to zero. The example shows an 8 marked as ON and a 2 marked as ON so we have 8 + 2 = 10.

Computers can't work with a decimal system because a current switch can only be either on or off, so there are only 2 choices.

These are the values in the decimal system:

10000000	1000000	100000	10000	1000	100	10	1

These are the values in the binary system:

128	64	32	16	8	4	2	1

Here, all the boxes are switched ON (11111111) which works out as:

$$1 + 2 + 4 + 8 + 16 + 32 + 64 + 128 = 255$$

128	64	32	16	8	4	2	1

Now add the zero option (00000000) and we have a possible 256 different numbers to play with.

These boxes are referred to as the data bus, and every single calculation that is made goes through this data bus. Collectively it is known as the Accumulator. (There is also one extra box that is used during the arithmetic process — the Carry Box).

Let's make our computer do something useful — let's add two numbers: 14 + 29.

First put 14 into the accumulator (in binary, as we have just seen).

8 + 4 + 2 or 00001110

128	64	32	16	8	4	2	1
				▓	▓	▓	

Next, overlay 29 into the accumulator: 16 + 8 + 4 + 1 or 00011101.

128	64	32	16	8	4	2	1
			▓	▓	▓		▓

Now mix the 2 binary codes on top of each other and apply a few rules. Start at the far right box and work to the left.

We do, though, need one extra ingredient — the Carry Box. This is another separate box that will be switched ON if the processor wants to remember something while it is doing its calculations.

The Carry Box starts in the OFF position. ☐

There are 4 rules that the transistors are made to follow:

1) 3 Boxes OFF = Leave all 3 OFF

☐   ☐   ☐
                                         Carry

2) 1 Box ON = Leave Box On, Carry Box OFF

▓   ☐   ☐
                                           Carry

3) 2 Boxes ON = Both OFF, Switch Carry Box ON

▓   ▓

☐   ☐   ▓
                                           Carry

4) 3 Boxes ON = Leave Boxes ON, Keep Carry Box ON

☐ ☐ ☐

Carry

When we press the "Equals" button these rules are executed starting from the far right box:

Box	Switch Position 1st Number (14)	Switch Position 2nd Number (29)	Carry to next Box	Apply the Rule	Acc Result
Box 1 Right	☐	▣	↓	1 ON	1
Box 2	▣	☐	☐	1 ON	1
Box 3	▣	▣	☐	2 ON	0
Box 4	▣	▣	▣	ALL 3 ON	1
Box 5	☐	▣	▣	2 ON	0
Box 6	☐	☐	▣	1 ON	1
Box 7	☐	☐	☐	NONE ON	0
Box 8 Left	☐	☐	☐	NONE ON	0

The first row of the table above, below the headings, is where the first sequence is carried out to calculate the answer (find the text 'Box 1 Right'). The next column to the right holds the first bit of the number 14 which is an empty box or a zero. Now go right to the next column to find the first bit of the number 29 which is an ON box or a one. The next column contains the result of the Carry Box which in this case is zero as it always will be for the very first sequence. Carry on right to the next column to see the rule applied which in this case is rule 2 or '1 Box ON' meaning that the first bit of the answer is an ON or a one (far right column). Note also that the Carry Box remains empty or zero as it is presented downwards for the next sequence. So the Accumulator result for the first bit or sequence is ON or one. Now start again at the left column 'Box 2' and repeat all the way down to the bottom of the table filling in the Accumulator result for each bit or sequence.

At the end, we see the accumulator is left with the right hand column, reading from the bottom upwards as 00101011

128	64	32	16	8	4	2	1

$$1 + 2 + 8 + 32 = 43$$

That is how a computer knows that 14 + 29 = 43. It simply goes through a process of shuffling boxes to come up with the correct answer, albeit at mind boggling speed.

But how do we actually get the computer to do this? We need a program that will sequentially run each instruction one by one until we get the required result. The accumulator, where we have just calculated the answer to our sum, can also be used to hold codes that are used as instructions. So the accumulator can receive an instruction code and then immediately afterwards receive the actual number (or data) required. This is the fundamental process of the computer:

1. DATA	Get a number (14)
2. INSTRUCTION	Apply an Adding process (+ button)
3. DATA	Get another number (29)
4. INSTRUCTION	Display the answer (= button)

Another instruction example could be to store a copy of the number you are working on (the one held in the accumulator) into memory so you can use it later. The CODE for 'send to memory' in the BBC computer is 141 (Decimal) or 10001101 (Binary). So this number is specially reserved for the action of — "take contents of accumulator and send to a memory address for storage."

128	64	32	16	8	4	2	1

1. DATA1 = &0DFF (The address 0DFF on the memory chip which I have labeled as DATA1 - we'll discuss addresses later)
2. LDA #14 (LoaD the Accumulator with the number [#] 14)
3. STA DATA1 (STore the contents of the Accumulator into the memory address DATA1 or 0DFF)

So the accumulator gets filled with 00001110 (14) and then the next instruction comes in as 10001101 ('send to memory') and it sends the 00001110 or decimal 14 to memory.

For completeness, the code for the addition (14 + 29) above is:

1. DATA1 = &0DFF (The address on the memory chip)
2. LDA #14 (Load the accumulator with number 14)
3. ADC #29 (Add the number 29 together with 14)
4. STA DATA1 (Store the contents of the accumulator into the memory address DATA1 0DFF)

(Note: there are many other considerations to be made for this code to work properly, like considering numbers greater than 256, but this demon-strates the fundamentals.)

Storing into Memory

The addressing system for memory is very similar but more memory boxes are required, as otherwise the computer would be so limited it would be useless. Therefore they allow not 8 boxes (bits), as in the accumulator, but 16 bits. The address on the memory chip we gave was 0DFF, which stands for quite a large number (3,583) and represents the number of the filing location.

0DFF is hexadecimal code, using 16 as the base; designed so that just 4 digits can represent a number as large as 65535, which obviously needs 5 digits. It does this by using letters, once you reach the number 10.

Decimal	1	2	3	4	5	6	7	8	9	10	11	12	13	14	15
Hex	1	2	3	4	5	6	7	8	9	A	B	C	D	E	F

With decimals, you need two digits to represent the numbers 10 to 15. With hexadecimal you only need one digit. This is the base 16 format (note 16 x 16 = 256)

4096	256	16	1
0	D	F	F

(O) x 4096 = 0
(D) or 13 x 256 = 3328
(F) or 15 x 16 = 240
(F) or 15 x 1 = 15

Added together you get 3,583 - or memory location 3,583. Only 4 digits required but remember we can now have an address FFFF, which gives a possible 65,535 addresses in only 4 digits. We now need to represent the 4 digit Hex code (ODFF) in binary format as a computer can only process numbers in ones or zeros:

Hex	0	D	F	F
Binary	0000	1101	1111	1111
Decimal (3,583)	0	3328	240	15

16 bit representation of 0DFF:

32768	16384	8192	4096	2048	1024	512	256	128	64	32	16	8	4	2	1

So going back to the sum we were working on earlier, the contents of the accumulator, 43 (00101011), goes off to the above memory location which we can consider as either of the following:

- Easy to understand, decimal placement number 3,583 (the 3,583rd box row in memory)

- Nonintuitive binary code (0000 1101 1111 1111)

- Hexadecimal, clever 4 digit representation 0DFF to help programmers write their code.

At this location, you will find an 8-bit set of boxes that holds the code 00101011 (43) and elsewhere in the computer it knows that the name associated with this address location (0DFF) is DATA1.

So we know how the computer does the calculations utilizing Instructions and Data. We also know how it stores the data and of course it does the opposite to retrieve the data. If you could see inside a section of RAM (Random Access Memory) it would look something like this - just a whole series of transistor boxes that are either ON or OFF in address order (note 0DFF contains the binary for our answer, 43):

0DFF								
0E00								
0E01								
0E02								
0E03								

Making choices

This ability is perhaps at the heart of all computing wizardry, the ability to make a choice. Now we can give a RAM address a specific number, we can compare it to another number stored at a separate address.

1. LDA #14 (Load the accumulator with number 14)

2. IF #14 ‹ #29 (If the number in the accumulator is less than 29)

3. THEN SUBTRACT #14 from #29 (if the condition above is met then subtract 14 from 29)

4. ELSE ADD #14 to #29 (if the condition above was not met, our program may crash if we create a negative number in the answer so in this case we should add the numbers to prevent a crash)

	128	64	32	16	8	4	2	1
14					▨	▨	▨	
29				▨	▨	▨		▨

The above example doesn't serve any real useful purpose but it does demonstrate the fundamental process. We can easily see how the number with the left most bit switched ON (16) must be bigger because all the binary numbers to the right cannot possibly add up to a greater number (8 + 4 + 2 + 1 = 15). Once we have this simple and quick ability to compare two data bits we can go on to create a very powerful machine that makes choices — but it's still only shuffling bits of data.

Writing a computer program

The list of steps for the computer to activate is of course the program. Each step is brought into the accumulator, one by one, from the memory (ROM or RAM). ROM (Read-Only Memory) is the location of the code written by the computer designer and this is loaded up when the computer is switched on to prepare the computer ready for use. The user cannot utilize this section of the memory — if he did, the computer would crash — it's like afflicting the computer with a stroke, it would not be able to function properly. RAM (Random Access Memory) is where the user's programs and data are stored which is brought into the accumulator step by step to be processed.

So, 8 bits of code come into the accumulator, it is told if it is an instruction code or a data code and acts accordingly. This carries on until the end of the program. The addition of 14 + 29 is really quite mechanical.

One instruction in low level languages (like Assembly Language we used above) corresponds to one instruction, like STA DATA1. A high level Language needs to be either compiled or interpreted. Compilers take the source code and translate the entirety of it into machine code now negating the use of the original program. Just like a page of text being translated from French to English in one go, once it is done there is no need to refer back to the French page.

Interpreters (Like BBC Basic which is a higher level than BBC Assembly language) take the source code and translate it into machine code but one line at a time so does need access to the original program to get the next line of code (easier to write but slower in operation). Just like a paragraph of text being translated from French to English, sentence by sentence, once one sentence is complete, there is a need to refer back to the French page to get the next sentence.

But all languages, whether low level assembly or high level BASIC end up as simple codes which are inserted into the accumulator one by one. And this has limitations. Keeping with the analogy of a spoken language but with a new rule that you have to pay me 5 cents for each word you use to instruct me, this is how you might go about getting me to make you a cheap cup of coffee.

    BOIL WATER
    GET CUP
    GET TEASPOON
    PUT COFFEE IN CUP
    POUR BOILING WATER
    STIR COFFEE

This would be assembly language. To make it into a higher level language it would simply consist of one instruction and would read:

    MAKE COFFEE (CUP)

Then, from this one command, the interpreter would go to various memory addresses and pull out these same individual instructions below, it's just that you wouldn't know it is happening:

BOIL WATER
GET CUP
GET TEASPOON
PUT COFFEE IN CUP
POUR BOILING WATER
STIR COFFEE

The reason it's called high level is that provided it is within the rules, I can also make subtle changes, for example by simply writing:

MAKE COFFEE (MUG)

Now the interpreter would go to the same memory addresses to pull out the individual instructions but would insert MUG instead of CUP:

BOIL WATER
GET CUP
GET TEASPOON
PUT COFFEE IN MUG
POUR BOILING WATER
STIR COFFEE

The most fundamental code that runs the BBC computer and indeed all computer systems is Machine Code which is at the top of this list and the lower you go in the list the higher the Language level or the more work is done for you behind the scenes:

Machine Code (Very hard)
Assembly Language (Hard)
C, FORTRAN, COBOL, Java
BASIC (Beginner's All-Purpose Symbolic Instruction Code)

Assembly Language and Machine code are specific to each make of processor chip, so it won't run on two different designs; and therefore it won't normally work on different brands of computer. This means you would have to learn different exceptions for each computer type. High-level languages are written to suit each different type of processor, allowing us to use the same form of language.

You can see how useful high-level programming languages are, as they are quick to write, pack in all the extra hidden lines of code, can be versatile (CUP or MUG) and work on all computers. The only catch is that the interpreting needs more lines of code, and thus more time to run, so the program becomes slower.

But processors get faster as the years go on, so not a problem...until the processor gets too hot because it is running so fast and melts... Now you need twin processors to share the task!

Appendix 2: Accident Statistics

Here is a table of worldwide passenger aircraft accidents involving fatalities for aircraft certified to carry at least 6 people, including crew (1945–
2019). When trying to draw conclusions from the data, there are several
factors to bear in mind. For one thing, in the early years there was less technology available to assist the pilots. At the same time, aircraft had a far lower
seating capacity, and there were not the high numbers of worldwide flights
we have today.

Year	Number of Accidents	Passenger Fatalities
2019	125	578
2018	115	1039
2017	102	399
2016	106	631
2015	127	904
2014	125	1329
2013	141	453
2012	156	800
2011	154	828
2010	162	1154
2009	161	1108
2008	190	902

Year	Number of Accidents	Passenger Fatalities
2007	169	984
2006	193	1303
2005	194	1463
2004	179	767
2003	201	1233
2002	198	1419
2001	210	1536
2000	196	1586
1999	221	1150
1998	225	1721
1997	232	1768
1996	250	2779
1995	266	1828
1994	231	2018
1993	275	1763
1992	265	2296
1991	259	2019
1990	281	1447
1989	337	2603
1988	306	2392
1987	341	2157
1986	276	1781
1985	296	3023
1984	284	1333
1983	289	2047
1982	309	2066
1981	320	1585
1980	379	2343
1979	381	2572
1978	408	2220
1977	373	2558
1976	308	2416
1975	332	1930
1974	316	2782

Year	Number of Accidents	Passenger Fatalities
1973	372	2975
1972	374	3316
1971	330	2304
1970	312	2188
1969	364	2752
1968	339	2433
1967	353	2351
1966	281	2222
1965	293	2272
1964	273	1803
1963	211	1838
1962	262	2477
1961	262	1962
1960	234	2033
1959	242	1524
1958	272	1808
1957	263	1654
1956	242	1434
1955	278	1423
1954	289	1549
1953	337	1970
1952	403	2284
1951	491	2304
1950	426	2138
1949	351	1916
1948	391	1978
1947	371	1922
1946	424	2064
1945	737	4660

Table of accidents in date order showing aircraft type and fatalities (2010–2019). This data is compiled from the official accident investigations by the pertinent authorities and was used to order the categories of accident in this book. Further information can be sought on-line by searching the aircraft type together with the accident date.

Year	Aircraft	Day	Fatalities
2019	Boeing 707-3J9C	January 14	15
2019	DC-3	January 21	2
2019	Convair C-131B	February 8	1
2019	Boeing 767-375	February 23	3
2019	Douglas DC-3	March 9	14
2019	Boeing 737 MAX 8	March 10	157
2019	Let L-410	April 14	2
2019	Sukhoi Superjet 100	May 5	41
2018	Antonov An-148	February 11	71
2018	ATR 72-200	February 18	66
2018	Bombardier Q400	March 12	51
2018	Boeing 737-700	April 17	1
2018	Boeing 737-200	May 18	112
2018	Bombardier Dash 8 Q400	August 10	1
2018	Boeing 737-800	September 28	1
2018	Boeing 737 MAX 8	October 29	189
2018	Boeing 757-200	November 9	1
2017	Boeing 747-400F	January 16	39
2017	Antonov An-26	April 29	8
2017	Let L-410	May 27	2
2017	Antonov An-26	October 14	4
2017	ATR 42-300	December 13	1
2017	Cessna 208 Caravan	December 31	12
2016	Bombardier CRJ200	January 8	2
2016	DHC-6 Twin Otter	February 24	23
2016	Antonov An-26	March 9	3
2016	Boeing 737-800	March 19	62

2016	Britten-Norman Islander	April 13	12
2016	Antonov An-12	May 18	7
2016	Airbus A320	May 19	66
2016	Boeing 777-300	August 3	1
2016	DHC-4T Turbo Caribou	October 31	4
2016	Avro RJ85	November 28	71
2016	ATR-42-500	December 7	47
2016	Boeing 727-200	December 20	5
2015	ATR-72	February 4	43
2015	Airbus A320	March 24	150
2015	Swearingen Metro II	April 13	2
2015	ATR-42	August 16	54
2015	DHC-6 Twin Otter	October 2	10
2015	Airbus A321	October 31	224
2015	Antonov An-12	November 4	41
2015	Airbus A310-300F	December 24	8
2014	DHC-6 Twin Otter	February 16	18
2014	Boeing 777	March 8	239
2014	Boeing 777	July 17	298
2014	ATR-72	July 23	48
2014	MD-83	July 24	116
2014	Antonov An-140	August 10	40
2014	Short 360	October 29	2
2014	Airbus A320	December 28	162
2013	Bombardier CRJ200	January 29	21
2013	Antonov An-24	February 13	5
2013	Beechcraft 1900C-1	March 8	2
2013	Boeing 747 freighter	April 29	7
2013	Boeing 777	July 6	3
2013	de Havilland DHC-3	July 7	10
2013	Airbus A300 freighter	August 14	2
2013	Embraer 120	October 3	16
2013	ATR-72	October 16	49

2013	Boeing 737	November 17	50
2013	Embraer 190	November 29	33
2012	ATR-72	April 2	33
2012	Boeing 737	April 20	127
2012	Sukhoi Superjet 100	May 9	45
2012	Dornier Do 228	May 14	15
2012	Boeing 727	June 2	12
2012	MD-83	June 3	153
2012	Antonov An-28	September 12	10
2012	Dornier Do 228	September 28	19
2012	Britten-Norman Islander	October 7	3
2012	Ilyushin Il-76T freighter	November 30	32
2012	Antonov An-26	December 17	4
2012	Fokker 100	December 25	2
2012	Tupolev Tu-204	December 29	5
2011	Tupolev Tu-154	January 1	3
2011	Boeing 727	January 9	78
2011	Fairchild Metroliner III	February 10	6
2011	Let L-410 Turbolet	February 14	14
2011	Antonov An-12	March 21	14
2011	Bombardier CRJ-100	April 4	32
2011	Xian MA60	May 7	25
2011	Saab 340	May 18	22
2011	Tupolev Tu-134	June 20	47
2011	Cessna 208 Caravan	July 4	1
2011	Ilyushin Il-76	July 6	9
2011	Boeing 727	July 8	77
2011	Antonov An-24	July 11	7
2011	Let L-410 Turbolet	July 13	16
2011	Boeing 747 freighter	July 28	2
2011	Antonov An-12	August 9	11
2011	Boeing 737	August 20	12

2011	Fairchild Metroliner III	September 6	8
2011	Yakovlev Yak-42	September 7	44
2011	Beechcraft 1900D	September 25	19
2011	CASA C-212 Aviocar	September 29	18
2011	de Havilland DHC-8	October 13	28
2011	Cessna 208 Grand	October 14	8
2010	Boeing 737-800	January 25	90
2010	Airbus A300B4F	April 13	7
2010	Airbus A330	May 12	103
2010	Antonov An-24	May 17	44
2010	Boeing 737-800	May 22	158
2010	CASA C-212 Aviocar	June 19	11
2010	Airbus A321	July 28	152
2010	Antonov An-24	August 3	12
2010	Boeing 737	August 16	2
2010	Embraer E-190	August 24	44
2010	Dornier Do 228	August 24	14
2010	Let L-410	August 25	20
2010	Boeing 747-400	September 3	2
2010	ATR-42	September 13	17
2010	ATR-72	November 4	68
2010	Beechcraft 1900	November 5	21
2010	Antonov An-24	November 11	6
2010	Ilyushin Il-76TD,	November 28	11
2010	Tupolev Tu-154	December 4	2
2010	DHC-6 Twin Otter	December 15	22

Image Credits

1. Illustration © Statista Airliner accident fatalities by year from 1972 to 2018.
   Illustration © Statista https://www.statista.com/chart/12393/2017-was-the-safest-year-in-the-history-of-air-travel
   https://creativecommons.org/licenses/by-nd/3.0/

2. Permission to reprint/use granted by the National Safety Council © 2020

3. B3A – Bureau of Aircraft Accidents Archives / Ronan HUBERT, Accidentologist

4. Left: Webernoid (pixabay.com)
   Right: Image by PublicDomainPictures from Pixabay

5. StuartBrady

6. Peter Collins

7. OpenClipart-Vectors (pixabay.com)

8. Freepik.com. This cover has been designed using resources from Freepik.com

9. Left: Shahram Sharifi - GNU Free Documentation License
   Right: Norio Nakayama
   https://creativecommons.org/licenses/by-sa/2.0/deed.en

10. FAA's "Lessons Learned from Civil Aviation Accidents" https://lessons-learned.faa.gov/

11. Image by 2234701 from Pixabay

12. James Wainscoat

13. Aircraft-cockpits.co.uk

14. user:Looie496

15. Clker-Free-Vector-Images (pixabay.com)

16. GNU Free Documentation License, Version 1.2

17. Peter Collins

18. Glosser.ca - https://creativecommons.org/licenses/by-sa/3.0/deed.en

19. Image courtesy of wikiHow.com from the article https://www.wikihow.com/Draw-an-Hourglass"

20. Grafiker61 - https://creativecommons.org/licenses/by-sa/4.0/deed.en

21. https://www.bea.aero/docspa/2009/f-cp090601.en/pdf/f-cp090601.en.pdf

22. Hardy Heinlin: www.aerowinx.com

23. Hardy Heinlin - www.aerowinx.com.

24. Cockpitrevolution.com/boeing747.html

25. Peter Collins

26. Peter Collins

27. Peter Collins

28. Peter Collins

29. Reproduced with permission of Jeppesen Sanderson, Inc.

30. Reproduced with permission of Jeppesen Sanderson, Inc.

31. Reproduced with permission of Jeppesen Sanderson, Inc.

32. Reproduced with permission of Jeppesen Sanderson, Inc.

33. Reproduced with permission of Jeppesen Sanderson, Inc.

34. https://www.flightsimulator.com

35. Reproduced with permission of Jeppesen Sanderson, Inc.

36. Reproduced with permission of Jeppesen Sanderson, Inc.

37. Reproduced with permission of Jeppesen Sanderson, Inc.

38. https://www.flightsimulator.com

39. http://movies.airclips.com/

40. Julien Scavini - https://creativecommons.org/licenses/by-sa/3.0/deed.en

41. Cockpitrevolution.com/boeing747.html

42. Peter Collins

43. Stuart Higgins - https://creativecommons.org/licenses/by-nd/4.0

44. Plastic Logic - https://creativecommons.org/licenses/by-sa/2.0/deed.en

45. Peter Collins

46. MdeVicente

47. Cockpitrevolution.com/boeing747.html

48. Benjamin Earwicker: FreeImages.com

49. mohamed_hassan (pixabay.com)

50. Martha Dominguez de Gouveia: Unsplash.com

51. ID 66366016 © Anton Samsonov | Dreamstime.com

52 12019 (pixabay.com)

53. Petr Pavlicek/IAEA — https://creativecommons.org/licenses/by-sa/2.0/deed.en

54. Freepik.com. This cover has been designed using resources from Freepik.com

55. DanielPenfield — https://creativecommons.org/licenses/by-sa/3.0/deed.en

56. Clker-Free-Vector-Images (pixabay.com)

57. SpaceX: Pexels.com

58. Alec Wilson: https://creativecommons.org/licenses/by-sa/2.0/deed.en

59. Davidelit

60. Andrew Heneen - https://creativecommons.org/licenses/by/3.0/deed.en

61. U.S. Navy photo courtesy of The Boeing Co.

Appendix: B3A — Bureau of Aircraft Accidents Archives / Ronan HUBERT, Accidentologist

Printed in the United States
By Bookmasters